The
Joy Ride

The Joy Ride

Everyday Ways to Lasting Happiness

Robert H. Lauer
&
Jeanette C. Lauer

DIMENSIONS
FOR LIVING

NASHVILLE

THE JOY RIDE
EVERYDAY WAYS TO LASTING HAPPINESS

Copyright © 1994 by Dimensions for Living

This book is printed on acid-free, recycled paper.

Library of Congress Cataloging-in-Publication Data

LAUER, ROBERT H.
    The joy ride / Robert H. Lauer, Jeanette C. Lauer.
    p.   cm
    ISBN 0-687-13053-0 (alk. paper)
    1. Joy—Religious aspects—Christianity. I. Lauer, Jeanette C.
II. Title.
BV4647.J68L38   1994
241'.4—dc20   93-8153
                                               CIP

Scripture quotations are from the New Revised Standard Version of the Bible, copyright © 1989 by the Division of Christian Education of the National Council of the Churches of Christ in the USA. Used by permission.

94 95 96 97 98 99 00 01 02 03 — 10 9 8 7 6 5 4 3 2 1
MANUFACTURED IN THE UNITED STATES OF AMERICA

To those who bring us joy

Jon, Kathy, Julie, Jeffrey, Kate, Jeff, and Krista

Contents

The
Joy Ride

PART I

Understanding Joy

Restore to me the joy of your salvation.

Psalm 51:12

"I have said these things to you so that my joy may be in you, and that your joy may be complete."

John 15:11

┌─────────────┐
│   │
│   1   │
│   │
└─────────────┘

Joy: The Elusive Emotion

——◆◆——

W e'll call him Bill. He was about twenty-four years of age. We were at a gathering for Christian young people. Bill introduced himself, then began to talk about his faith. We found his discussion unsettling, particularly when he said: "It is so great to have the peace and joy of God's salvation." We didn't disagree with the statement. But nonverbally, Bill was telling us a different story. He spoke about joy, but his sad face and slumped posture provided a contrary message. Looking at him without hearing his words, you would have thought he was discussing some serious problems in his life. Bill's words expressed gratitude for joy; his face and body communicated spiritual depression.

To be sure, Bill knew that one of the promises God gives to his people is joy in life. "With joy," cried Isaiah, "you will draw water from the wells of salvation" (12:3). The Hebrew word that is translated "joy" here refers to an emotion of soaring; it means joy, gladness, and exultation. Biblical joy is the human spirit stretching to the limits, bursting out of all earthly confines, dancing in the heavens.

This is what Bill wanted, but what he clearly didn't have. He wanted to live a life that soared. He wanted to experience for himself the fulfillment of Christ's words: "I came that they may have life, and have it abundantly" (John 10:10). Yet Bill was clearly gripped by the hands of melancholy.

Joy Is Elusive

Was Bill so unusual in claiming to possess a joy that obviously had eluded him? Don't many Christians today similarly find joy elusive? Some years ago the famed English preacher D. Martyn Lloyd-Jones gave a series of sermons on spiritual depression. His first sermon on the topic was based on the psalmist's question: "Why are you cast down, O my soul?" He noted the frequency with which the issue is raised in the Scriptures and said we can only conclude that it is a very common condition. Indeed, Dr. Lloyd-Jones said he himself had observed a large number of unhappy Christians. Too often, he pointed out, Christians are stuck "in the doldrums," look unhappy, and lack joy. And the effect of that joylessness is that many people lose interest in the Christian faith.

We, too, have been struck by the number of Christians who seem to find joy elusive. The problem was dramatized for us by a pastor who told us that he was startled one day into the realization that he was missing the joy he had been preaching about to others. He was talking to a woman in his congregation about one of the programs of the church. "It will bring a lot of joy to those who participate," he told her. She hesitated a moment, then said: "Pastor, how are things with you? You look so gloomy when you're sitting in your pulpit chair waiting to preach."

"Although her statement shocked me," the pastor told us, "I knew she was right. I didn't admit it to her, but I admitted it to myself. The joy I preached about was missing from my own life." Two things need to be said here.

First, if there is little joy in your life, or not as much as you would like to have, you are missing some of the richer facets of God's salvation. You are not soaring as often as you could or as often as God would have you.

Second, note that we tie joy to God's salvation. Clearly, people who are not Christians also have joy, and they have it in some of the same kinds of experiences we describe in this book. But we believe there is a qualitative difference to Christian joy, a difference that can best be described as joy in the context of the embrace of God. In relating all things back to God, Christians add a new dimension to experience.

For instance, it is one thing to stand on a mountaintop and look with awe-adorned joy at the world around you. It is a leap into a new dimension of joy to view the same scene knowing that you are in the embrace of God and looking at his awesome creation. In like manner, it is one thing to joyously witness the birth of a child. It is a leap into a new dimension to be aware that you are embraced by God as you witness a new gift of life that he has entrusted to the world.

When you are aware that your life is circumscribed by God, even problems and suffering have a different meaning. For non-Christians, joy may be pushed aside by the difficult times. This is not necessarily true for Christians. Thus, Jesus "for the sake of the joy that was set before him endured the cross" (Heb. 12:2). Paul wrote to the Philippians about his joy even though he was in prison. And James counsels us to "consider it nothing but joy" when we "face trials of any kind" (James 1:2).

A German who was put into prison for opposing Hitler wrote to his wife that, though it sounded strange, he had learned one thing in prison—to be joyful! The joy came as he grew conscious of the presence of God. This does not mean he no longer suffered. As Peter pointed out, we can rejoice in our hope "even if now for a little while you have had to suffer various trials" (1 Peter 1:6). Christian joy neither dispels all suffering nor demands the absence of suffering.

As a Christian, then, you can miss out on a good deal of joy. Or you can have joyous experiences like others. Or you can add a new dimension of intensity and meaning to your joys and all other experiences by remembering that you are in the embrace of God. Our purpose is to help you increase joyous experiences in your life. Our assumption is that you will intensify those experiences by remembering who you are—God's own child, redeemed and possessed by Jesus Christ the Lord, whose love is unfailing.

There Are Obstacles to Joy

One reason Christians miss out on joy is the nature of the world in which we live. A number of observers have pointed out that dark clouds hang over the psyche of more and more people. Of course, gloomy assessments of human life are not new. In his novel *Candide,* Voltaire had one of his characters say that humans are born "to live either in the convulsions of distress or the lethargy of boredom." Today, we could add "the muck of melancholy" to the list.

Some researchers have labeled the 1990s the "gray nineties." The label is based on the alarming increase in depression in the last two decades, particularly among the nation's youth. The rise in rates of depression began in the 1970s. Interestingly, it is among those born after World War II, the Baby Boomers, that the problem is particularly acute. The Baby Boomers have higher rates of depression, and they suffer from it at an earlier age than did previous generations; in fact, they are ten times more likely to be depressed than are their parents and grandparents.

The Joy Ride

In addition to the increased rates of depression, there are other signs of our emotional affliction. Depression is linked with suicide. The overall suicide rate in the nation has also risen over the past two decades. The rate rose only for children and young adults, however; it declined for older people. Again, it is the Baby Boomers who seem to be suffering the most. Along with depression and suicide, there is a litany of other woes that we could discuss—drug and alcohol abuse, violence, cynicism, declining confidence in leaders, the lack of heroes among the young, and such new afflictions as the Chronic Fatigue Syndrome that strikes most often at young, white professionals and leaves them listless every day of their lives.

It didn't surprise us when, sitting in a meeting of professionals who were planning a family life conference, a physician blurted out: "Is anyone today really happy? I see very few people in my practice that I would call happy anymore." Like other observers, he had a sense that American society has slipped into an age of melancholy, and he saw one of the consequences in the changed mood of his patients.

The web of melancholy that has settled over our age can entangle Christians as well as others. It is true, of course, that Christians of every generation have had to cope with a world troubled in one way or another. And we suspect that Christians of every generation have had to wrestle with the same problem of keeping themselves from being infected with the despair around them.

One of the problems today is that we seem at best to tumble from one problem to another and at worst to be losing ground in more areas than we are making progress. Living in an age of increased difficulties of every kind, then, Christians may find themselves spending more time doing battle with the demons of gloom than in rejoicing in the life that God has given them.

There is a story that seems to reflect the feeling that

many people have about life today. The story concerns a couple buying a toy for their young son. The salesperson assured them that he had just the thing: "It's a puzzle that will help your child adapt to modern life. Any way he puts it together, it's wrong."

In addition to the nature of our world, there is another, more subtle, obstacle. All of the major sources of joy are also sources, or potential sources, of pain. You might be tempted to skip the possibility of joy in order to avoid the potential for pain. Marriage can be a source of joy, for example. Yet, as anyone who is separated or divorced can tell you, it can also cause years of agony.

What we are saying, then, is that in order to have more joy in your life, you have to be willing to take certain risks. We were once in the Blue Ridge mountains, looking forward to a spectacular view from a particular high point. When we got there, however, we found the area below us shrouded in fog. On another day, we would have experienced the joy of looking out over God's great creation. On that day, we left empty and frustrated.

That's the way it is with joy. Whenever you engage in something that has the potential for being joyous, you also run the risk of disappointment or even pain. Some people never hike in the mountains because they're afraid of poison ivy or snakes. Some people forgo marriage because they came from a broken home and don't want to repeat the painful experience. Some people never further their education because they don't want to risk the possibility of failure.

Realistically, every experience that has the potential for joy also carries certain risks. Still, to forgo the potential joy in order to avoid the possibility of pain is to engage in what novelist Edith Wharton called a "desultory dabbling with life."

We once saw in a gift shop an item called "instant

infant." It was a large cardboard baby. The label noted that you could now have your own baby without all the pain of pregnancy, childbirth, nighttime feedings, diaper changing, and so on. Instant infant carries no risks. Neither does it bring any joy.

Joy Is Part of God's Treasure for Christians

What exactly is this joy that causes us to be willing to take risks? The nine different biblical words that are translated "joy" can also mean such things as gladness, mirth, and exultation. But what actually happens to you when you experience joy? We asked the question of hundreds of Christians who then told us about a joyous experience. Fortunately, we didn't get hundreds of different answers. People agreed that joy is an experience of intense happiness *plus much more.* Listen to some of the responses; you can feel the intensity of the emotion:

• "Joy is happiness. But it is more. It is a feeling of being intensely overwhelmed. It is an experience of incredible fullness and pleasure; a spiritual awareness that something has entered your soul, and you know that you will never be the same again."
• "Happiness is a part of joy, but in addition there is a strong sense of being part of things, of being alive, of sensing the meaning of the universe, of well-being and vitality. There is also a sense of being swept along by the force of God. When I have joy, I am at peace with God, with nature, with life, and with myself."
• "Joy is a feeling of pleasure. And the degree of intensity and breadth of the feeling can vary from mild to a state of being engulfed in what can be called ecstasy. And like all feelings, it can be experienced in the body as well as in the mind. For me, a basic component of joy is beauty."

• "Joy is a feeling that uplifts the spirit, pushes negative thoughts to the sideline. Joy makes me feel great. Joy is total happiness."
• "Joy is that exhilarating feeling of pleasure, kind of like a natural high. It's an exciting, happy feeling of accomplishment, contentment, satisfaction, pride, sharing, loving, and of being loved."

So joy is powerful. It is like an emotional cornucopia, offering us a wealth of feelings that will enhance our lives. It is an intoxicating, addictive experience that makes us thirst for more. It is a part of the treasure that God promises to those who come to him. "I never experience it enough," one man told us. "I know you can't have joy all of the time, but I think I would like to anyway."

Joy is addictive because of all the "pluses" it adds to happiness. Sometimes the plus is a sense of peace. Sometimes it is a feeling of excitement or ecstasy or of being one with the entire universe. When you experience joy, you may feel serene, or you may want to jump and leap. You probably will feel good about yourself and the world in which you live. You may have an overwhelming sense of gratitude for God's gift of life. In any case, joy is a set of feelings that are so exhilarating to your spirit that you will want to experience it repeatedly.

Note that we said you may feel serene in a joyous experience. Do exhilaration and serenity seem contradictory? Actually, they are not, as Stephanie, a twenty-five-year-old travel agent, assured us. Stephanie told us that to her joy means "great happiness and elation, but yet it is more. It is deeper. It is a feeling in which I am in a state of complete peace with myself and my surroundings." She struggled a bit to expand her definition, then said exuberantly, "Let me tell you about a terrific experience that I consider to be one of joy. That's the best way I know to define it." Stephanie's experience occurred during the summer of her junior year in college. She was backpacking in Europe with a friend:

> I grew up in the Midwest. I had never spent any time around mountains until this trip. We were in Switzerland at the time and decided to go on a day hike in the mountains. As we climbed, I felt wonderful. It was a beautiful, sunny day. After a couple of hours, we took a break and sat down. And that's when I experienced the feeling of joy.
>
> "I looked around and realized I was completely surrounded by the Alps. I was totally taken in by the beauty of God's creation. As I scanned the mountains, I felt absolute peace within me. I can't ever remember a time when I felt so calm, so serene. I was in a state of real bliss, of pure joy. I felt at one with myself and with nature."

In contrast to Stephanie's experience of serene joy, Frances, a high school teacher, had a leaping experience. Frances defined joy as "an overwhelming emotion of delight." She went on to say that she feels joy is such a subjective experience that it is easier to talk about the event than to come up with a definition.

The experience of joy that Frances chose to share with us occurred some years earlier. It is embedded in her memory as one of the highest points of her life. At the time, she had been married for twenty years and was the mother of five children. Four years before the joyous event, she had decided to go to college, earn a degree, and become a teacher. Her experience of joy happened at her graduation, but not quite in the way she would have expected:

> "I remember watching my classmates receive their diplomas and how pleased I felt for them. Then it was my turn. I heard my name called. I rose and walked across the stage, concentrating on my footing so I wouldn't

stumble. Suddenly, through the silence of the crowd, I heard a loud male voice cry out: 'That's my mom!' A rumble of laughter and then warm applause from the audience followed my son's shout. My heart leapt with joy. My son had said more than those few words that still echo in my memory. What his words said to me was: 'Mom, I love you and I'm proud of you.'"

Frances paused. Clearly, she reexperienced the joy of the moment as she told the story. Then she went on to explain why it meant so much to her:

"My son was eighteen at the time. The reason I felt so incredibly joyous was that he is an adopted child, and his teenage years were very difficult ones for both of us. I had even begun to wonder about his attachment to our family. Those three words—'that's my mom!'—took away all my doubts. He was truly my son. He cared for me. He loved me. For years afterward, if we had any difficulties I would remember that moment and say to myself, 'That's my son. I know he loves me.'"

Joy, then, may be experienced in a variety of ways. But it is always a time of intense happiness along with other positive feelings. And it takes on a new dimension to the extent that one is aware of being in the embrace of God. It isn't necessary to always articulate that fact. Frances, for example, didn't have to say, "That's my son, whom God has given me." A silent "thank you, Father" would convey her sense of being one who is in Christ and who lives in the embrace of God.

You Can Find Joy

The biblical message is one of freely available joy. As Jesus said, "I have said these things to you so that my joy may be in you, and that your joy may be complete" (John 15:11). The hundreds of people who shared their joyous experiences with us corroborate the message that there is a wealth of joyous events that are available to every Christian.

Consider the story of Martin, a thirty-four-year-old artist. Martin believes that joy is both central and accessible to us. However, he hasn't always felt that way. It took a rather unusual and transforming experience to change his mind and his life. In fact, at the time his story began, he was captive to melancholy:

> "Although I would have denied it at the time, I was living with a vague feeling of dissatisfaction with life. I wasn't really engaged with life. My life was a little gloomy, like an overcast day. I was sitting on the sidelines, watching the world go by."

At the time, Martin's parents owned a vacation home near the confluence of two rivers. They used it to celebrate birthdays and other special occasions. It had a lot of good memories for Martin. Although his father owned it, Martin was responsible for its upkeep. In return, he could have his friends there, and use it as his personal "secluded, warm haven."

But one January his haven was taken from him. Torrential rains flooded the rivers and blocked the roads. The cabin was inaccessible. Martin agonized:

> "It was late February before I could get there again. I was shocked. Nothing was left. The cabin was destroyed. All of the trees and plants we had put in were gone or dead. A thick layer of dried mud covered the land. My green paradise was nothing more than a barren mud flat. Only a few of the trees that were there before my father bought the land still stood. They looked like mourners standing in a field of death.

"I went into a period of grieving. It was like a close and dear friend had died. I was still depressed and trying to understand it all when I went back in April. But this time, I was startled. Many of the trees showed signs of life. A bud here. A leaf there. I was overwhelmed by feelings of joy, struck by the fact that life was there after all! I felt lighter, as if I had lost some weight. The whole world was transformed. Colors were brighter. Sounds were more melodious. People were more beautiful. It came to me that God has a purpose for this world and that I am part of something that is bigger, wiser, and more lasting than I am."

Martin's feeling of joy lasted for a month. It was the beginning of a number of similar experiences. His attitude toward life changed dramatically. He stopped being a bystander and started being a participant.

Like Martin, you can find joy. O. Henry wrote that life is composed of sobs, sniffles, and smiles, with sniffles predominating. The biblical response is that God wills smiles more than sniffles and sobs. And the stories of Stephanie, Frances, and Martin illustrate the truth of the biblical answer. Modern life does not have to be set in a minor key. Joy can be more than a rare or nonexistent experience for you.

We want to repeat that finding joy does not depend on the absence of problems. Among those who shared joyous experiences with us, and who told us that joy was a crucial part of their lives, were a young mother who had been severely abused as a child by her parents, a middle-aged man who had lost a brother he deeply loved to a fatal disease, and a man who had a transforming experience of joy shortly after a painful breakup with a woman he loved.

Like others, Christians go through turbulent and painful times. Unlike others, Christians have a hope that cannot be fully crushed. And that means that nothing can irrevocably or indefinitely sever us from joy. We do not take lightly the distress of troubled times, but our purpose is to focus on joy.

The joyous celebration of life is not beyond the reach of any of us. The grace of God extends our reach so that we need not fall short of Christ's promise of life to the fullest. The crucial question is How? How can we each freely and joyously draw water from the wells of salvation? To raise the question is to make the assumption that joy is more than an automatic by-product of faith.

Some Christians with whom we have spoken insist that the Bible teaches that we should experience joy continually. If so, we have a long record of God's people who fall short of that ideal: David's distress, Elijah's despairing request for death, the psalmist's disclosure of his depression, Peter's anguish over being told to fellowship with Gentiles, and Paul's agony over the failings of his converts—all illustrate the dark side upon which every one of us necessarily walks at times.

Clearly, even Christ did not experience uninterrupted joy in his life. Nor did any of the people of God in the Scriptures. Nor did any Christian throughout history for whom we have biographical information. Joy, then, is not automatically and always ours simply because we believe. Rather, for the Christian, joy is an ever-present resource into which we can always tap in order to construct renewing experiences.

In other words, joy is always there to be claimed, though it is not always experienced. The challenge, then, is to learn how to experience joy more frequently. Or, phrased somewhat differently, the challenge is to increase the number of your joyous experiences. To do that, you need to know where to find joy. We will explore some of these places after we look more fully at the rewards of joy.

2

The Rewards of Joy

———◆———

Can you exist without joy? Of course. But you can't really *live.* As a woman told us: "Joy helps me feel complete. It is a necessary part of living a full life." Likewise, a man declared that joy "is a basic, innate need. Joy belongs to the side of us that is closest to the image of God. Where God is, peace and joy prevail, and that's the place I most long to be."

Compare those statements with that of a fifty-year-old real-estate broker who summed up his philosophy of life for us in two sentences: "Life is hard. And then you die." With a number of misfortunes in his life and no faith to sustain him, the broker looked bleakly at both his past and his future. He exists, but he doesn't really live, for he lacks the joy necessary to "have life, and have it abundantly" (John 10:10).

Joy facilitates our quest for fullness of life. It is an energizing, life-affirming emotion. Before we look at the ways to cultivate joy, let us consider the rewards of increasing the joy in one's life.

Joy Gives Meaning and Purpose to Life

"When I feel joy, I feel that my life has meaning and purpose," a legal secretary told us. "I feel that I am not alone in the world. I feel a sense of belonging and relatedness to others." She knows how crucial joy is for us. She knows why Jesus taught us that it is important "that my joy may be in you, and that your joy may be complete" (John 15:11).

Obviously, you can't feel joy all of the time. But when it comes, you have a sense that this is what life is all about. This feeling comes about because joy simultaneously links us with our world and our God. It is as though in joy we are standing with one foot on earth and one foot in heaven, and fully experiencing the richness of each. One person told us that joy provided him "with a glimpse of the eternal." Another said that joy "is like taking a dip into another world."

Of course, it isn't merely the joy itself but the joyous experience that gives meaning and purpose to life. It is when we have some kind of experience that is bathed in joy that we feel most fully engaged with life.

Eric is a teacher in the Midwest. Now in his thirties, he told us about a joyous experience that made him feel "incredibly rich." He was taking an early morning walk on an exquisite spring day. His thoughts progressed from "this is a beautiful day" to "this is the day the Lord made" to "this is God's world that I am enjoying." At that moment he had a sense of God's nearness. He felt joyous, and his thoughts continued:

"I realized that I am a part of God's world. The joy kind of sealed me into his plan. I knew that all I wanted was to fulfill his will for my life. And that I will be incredibly blessed if I just keep trying to follow his leading."

Joy Gives Us a Sense of Control

Psychologists emphasize that it is important to our health for us to have some sense of control over our lives.

Joy helps us to have that sense of control. For one thing, joy provides us with an escape from some of the vexing problems and situations that we all face. For a time, at least, we transcend them. We conquer them. And that means that we do have some control. Like the apostles who went their way rejoicing after being flogged and warned not to speak about Jesus Christ (Acts 5:41), we know that ultimately there is no problem and no situation that can separate us from the love of God.

The testimony of a church organist captures well the sense of control that comes with joy. He said, "When I feel joy, I am on top of the world and everything is going my way." While the joy lasts, he asserted, "all the bad things that could happen to me are blotted out, and all that I see and feel is the elation of the moment."

This sense of control can be particularly important when you face crises in your life. Thirty-nine-year-old Lindsay had learned through a number of joyous experiences that she had some control over her life. Her sense of control was not based on her own powers. Rather, like Paul, she believed that the same Christ who had brought her joy would give her the strength to do all things and meet all challenges (Phil. 4:13).

Lindsay's faith was put to a severe test. After a medical checkup, she was shocked to learn that she needed open-heart surgery. It was, she thought, the sort of thing that happened to others rather than to her—certainly to older people, but not to someone her age. Yet her physician insisted that it was a matter of life and death for her. "I got very angry," she said, "at suddenly being completely out of control over my body and the doctors and the technology."

Reminding herself of her Lord's promise, she fought to overcome her anger and regain control. She explained: "I decided that I would look at it this way: I am using the

doctors and the technology to control my own health."
The doctors weren't in control of her; she and God were
in control *of them.* Five weeks after the surgery, Lindsay
was back at work. "I remember the surge of elation and
the anticipation of a healthy life," she said. "It was a great
victory."

Lindsay's final words to us were these: "When you
have joy, you know that you can master life. Without joy,
people act like victims of their world. I don't want to be a
victim. I want to be a victor."

Joy Provides a Feeling of Well-being

Some years ago, when we were living in the Midwest,
a local radio personality had, as a regular guest on his
program, a cleaning lady who worked at the station.
They would chat on the air for a while, and then she
would conclude the interview with a resounding: "All is
well." He had heard her use these words one day to
reassure someone at the station and was so struck by
the force and sincerity of her words that he invited her
to be on his show. She listened to callers' problems and
provided down-to-earth advice. And, at the end of the
program, she always gave her final message: "All is
well."

She had a feeling of well-being. All is well. That didn't
mean that she had no problems. It didn't mean that she
never agonized or grieved or worried or felt low. She had
known all of these. But after sifting through the unsettling
and painful experiences, she clung to a firm belief that
with God's help she could handle whatever life brought
her. As a woman of faith, she knew that much of what
occurred in her life would be good and that there would
be many joyous experiences.

A feeling of well-being is something to be treasured.
Like the sense of control, it enables us to be healthier and

to function better in whatever we do. Joyous experiences help to develop that feeling of well-being. Joy, as one woman put it, is like a "natural high." A sense of well-being is the aftermath of that natural high.

It doesn't take a dramatic joyous incident in order to produce an aftermath of good feeling. A mother told us of "ordinary-life events" that brought much joy to her life. They included the laughter of children and various aspects of nature:

"I find beautiful sunsets a joy to watch. Nature fascinates me. Especially marine life. When I visit an aquarium and look at all of the beautiful fish, I think that they could only have been designed by God. And I realize how humble I am and how lucky I am that I can be there and enjoy such beauty. It's really an intense moment for me. And it stays with me."

A sense of well-being, then, seems to be an expected aftereffect of a joyous experience. There are specific ways in which joy leads to well-being. Some people pointed out that joy makes life more pleasant, that it adds light and carefree times that make us feel good generally. Others told us that joy tends to create a healthy mental state, a sense that "everything is in the right place."

A middle-aged man recognized the value of joy for mental health when he said:

"Joy keeps me healthy. When things do not go well, and I start to feel sad, I weigh the good things in my life and reflect on how fortunate I am. Sad feelings slowly lift, and I am able to regain a sense of joy for the things I really cherish—my marriage, my grandchildren, my career. Joy is a powerful ally in my life."

Indeed, joy is a powerful ally for any of us. Positive

emotions and moods generally make significant contributions to our well-being. Researchers tell us that joyous people are more positive in their interpretation of social situations, less hostile, and less anxious than people who are not joyous.

Another important way that a joyous experience can increase your well-being is to raise your self-esteem. As mentioned earlier, the joyous incident need not be a dramatic one to have a positive outcome. Meg, a graduate student, felt joy and an elevated self-esteem when her mother gave her a gift of a pearl ring. Her father had given the ring to her mother before Meg was born. What did that gift mean? To Meg it meant that her mother had entrusted the family heritage to her. She explained, "It gave me a new sense of how much she loves and trusts me. The ring reminds me that I'm someone special. It makes me feel good about myself."

Finally, joyous experiences increase our sense of well-being because there is frequently a sense of calmness and peace in the aftermath of the event. It is good to be "high." It is also good to be serene. The high of a joyous experience can often give way to a mood of serenity, as it did for Courtney, a twenty-nine-year-old ski enthusiast. After a particularly thrilling run down the slopes, she felt exhilarated for days. Then the exhilaration faded away. Instead of a loss, however, Courtney made a discovery:

> "I felt at peace with myself and my world. I think that was the first time that I realized that when joy goes away it doesn't leave you empty. You keep reaping the benefits even when the feelings change, because the new feelings are good ones too. It makes me feel energized. I want to help others to gain that kind of peace and health."

The Joy Ride

Joy Helps Us Through Difficult Times

Remember the real-estate broker? "Life is hard. And then you die." The broker was at least partly correct. Life *is* sometimes hard. There are difficult times. There are days when you don't want to get out of bed or leave for work. There are periods of life that you wish you could just skip over. There are words said and acts committed that you wish could be erased and reprogrammed like a videotape. There are seasons of stress, sometimes compounded by not just one but numerous things going wrong in your life.

But life isn't all sobs and sniffles and yawns. Indeed, it can't be, or we would all become self-destructive. Fortunately, there is also enjoyment and exhilaration. And it is the joyous experiences that strengthen us during the bleak times and motivate us to continue our pursuit of happiness and fulfillment. Joyous moments uplift our spirits, improve our general mood, and help us to keep in mind that life has its share of rainbows as well as storms.

We like to think of it in terms of emotional capital, which is the counterpart to the "emotional slush" that therapists talk about. *Emotional slush* refers to the hurts of the past that are not fully healed and that continue to vex us in various ways. *Emotional capital* refers to the reservoir of strength we have as a result of the joys of the past. Every new experience of joy adds to the emotional capital. And we can draw on that capital whenever we face difficult situations.

A family therapist told us that she periodically goes through times of turmoil when she questions her capacity to keep helping people. When that happens, she recalls the various joyous experiences of her life:

"Previous joyous experiences induce a pleasant feeling. Sometimes I can even recapture the joy I felt. Those experiences have left a positive residue that enables me to feel better about people and situations. I believe that the more I experience joy, the less I am troubled or stressed."

The therapist has learned to draw effectively on her emotional capital. She can't escape the troublesome times, but she knows the crucial importance of joyous experiences in dealing effectively with those times.

The power of joyous experiences to enable us in dealing with life's difficulties is enhanced if, like the therapist, we consciously remind ourselves of those experiences. The power is available even to those who face difficulties on a daily basis. Consider, for instance, a job that is literally one emergency after another—that of a paramedic.

Jed is a paramedic who knows well the stress of failed efforts to help people. "There are plenty of calls," he noted, "where you're too late . . . where things just don't work out." If his work was always like that, he admitted, he couldn't continue in it. But he told us about other kinds of calls:

"You really help somebody. You save someone's life or you bring relief to someone. I feel joy in those times. It's the joyous ones that keep me going. I keep those in mind and tell myself that they are what makes life worth living."

Jed, too, has found the value of joyous experiences in building up his emotional capital. And he knows how to draw on that capital to deal with the stresses of his life. You can do it as well.

Joy Helps Us Through Low Times

There are times when life is not particularly difficult but not particularly exciting either. These are the humdrum days that we plod through and shrug off as an inevitable part of living. Sometimes it isn't that we face a situation that repels us, but merely one that has no attraction. Sometimes we are not under great stress or distress, but are merely enduring some of the numerous small disappointments that are the common lot of humans.

One of the more perceptive of the people who shared their experiences of joy with us was Justin, a forty-year-old artist. Justin recognizes that life inevitably has its cycles of highs and lows, and that the cycles are to be received gladly rather than scorned as a cruel joke that God has played on us. He does not believe that it would be good for us to always be on a high plane. Joy and disappointment, he insists, "are both essential in learning the lessons of life."

Justin said that he has felt the "exuberant, inundating, renewing impact of joy," which has helped him through the disappointing times. An experience of joy that has sustained him through many discouraging moments occurred when he graduated from high school. While receiving his diploma, he heard the principal announce that he had achieved the salutatorian rank in his class. He knew that he had ranked in the top 5 percent, but the principal did not reveal the specific ranking until the exercises.

The award meant that Justin would get a full academic college scholarship. According to Justin, the elation he felt at the announcement "was intensified by the standing ovation of my friends, teachers, and parents." Justin continued to feel something of the elation throughout the summer because people in the community would stop and congratulate him wherever he happened to be. "Even at this moment," he told us, "I can feel the elation that engulfed me."

Justin continues to have his share of joyous and disappointing experiences, but when the disappointments come, he remembers the joys. And they sustain him. Citing the fact that Babe Ruth struck out more times at bat than he hit home runs, Justin said, "If you remember the home runs instead of the strike outs, it gives you strength to continue on when you walk away from the plate after another strike out. That's what joy does in my life. It keeps me going during those strike-out times."

Joy Energizes and Motivates

Joy energizes us for the business of life. It motivates us by giving specific direction or redirection to our lives. We tend to respond to joy and follow it avidly. In the case of William, a joyous experience gave his life a direction that neither he nor anyone in his family would have expected.

William grew up in a poor family, but his father managed to save enough money to send him to a Christian school. It was a highly competitive, multiracial school that demanded much from its students.

By the tenth grade, some of the pupils in William's class had already formed ideas of what they wanted to do in life, but he seemed to have no ambition. In fact, he disliked school and was often depressed. He worked hard, though, because he was aware of the sacrifice his family was making.

To encourage achievement, the school gave awards at the end of each semester. William was overwhelmed when his teacher announced his name as the winner of an award in public speaking. The teacher handed William a book and a certificate as his award, and said to him, "You know, I once had a great teacher by the name of William. I hope you can follow in his footsteps."

William told us that he accepted his award wordlessly:

"I was so surprised, I couldn't say anything. Not even thank you. I kept hearing the words over and over again: 'I hope you can follow in his footsteps.' I was filled with joy. I couldn't wait to go home and tell my parents."

When William proudly showed his parents his award, his mother shared a story with him he had never heard before. His great grandfather had been a teacher. He was still alive when William was born, and he told William's mother that he had prayed to God that William would be in love with knowledge. "Your great grandfather's prayer has been answered," she said to William.

William now knew what he wanted to do. He, too, would be an educator. He would go to college and prepare himself. As it turned out, he went even farther than he expected at the time—through graduate school and a doctoral degree. Joy took a listless young man and turned him into a scholar, an achiever. Joy motivated him to pursue academic and career excellence. Joy gave him direction and purpose. "With each bit of success in my work," he concluded, "I feel a renewed sense of joy not only for myself but for my parents and my great grandfather."

Joy Aids Personal Growth

To be fully alive is to grow. Those who get the most out of life are those who keep on growing—that is, they keep increasing their capacity to relate warmly and intimately with others. They continue to expand their ability to accept themselves and other people. And joy is a resource in accomplishing these tasks. It helps us to grow in at least four ways:

1. Joy changes us. As one man said, "Life will never be the same. If you truly experience joy, something new and significant has taken place." Hue, a young Asian American pianist, has been a Christian for just three years. Within the first year of her life as a Christian, a joyous experience changed her.

Hue had a friend who disappointed her by being very critical of Hue. But when Hue struggled with a bout of depression, her friend became very loving and caring. She explained:

"For the first time, I saw her as a real person, with both positive and negative qualities. It was a joyful experience for me. Seeing her in a new way made me a new person. I am better able to accept people, because we are all a mix of good and bad. The joy of that experience helped me to trust people more."

2. Joy makes us feel more complete. Many people struggle with a sense of being incomplete in some way. "God isn't finished with me yet" is a way of saying that we as Christians also are striving to be more complete. And joy is one of the ways that God puts his finishing touches on us.

Guy, a physician in a large metropolitan area, thought he had his life pretty well put together until a joyous event brought him to an abrupt turning point. He has been a physician for over twenty-five years, "intimately involved in life-and-death situations," as he put it. He has watched both birth and death with a certain amount of professional detachment: "Of course, I was happy when a baby safely made it into the world, and sometimes I felt like a failure when I was not able to keep a person alive. But these events were part of my work and fairly routine."

It all changed with Chelsey, his first grandchild. He was present when she was born. But this time, he was there as the father of the expectant mother and not as a doctor. He described how his professional "cool" vanished:

"It was incredible. I absolutely paid no notice to the medical aspects of the birth. What captured my attention was the courage and determination of my daughter as she pushed this new life into the world. And that tiny, wrinkled little girl—her perfection and the perfection of the moment took my breath away. I want you to know this unflappable M.D. was overcome with emotion and with a sense of the most exquisite joy."

The memory of that joy is still with Guy even though Chelsey is now three. The experience unleashed a part of him that he had never even known existed. He no longer feels compelled to hide his emotions. "In fact, it doesn't even embarrass me to sniffle during a sentimental movie," he told us.

For many people like Guy, an experience of joy has revealed unknown aspects of themselves or has empowered them to use their abilities in ways that they would never have had the courage to do. In the process, they have become more fully the persons that God intended them to be. In a real sense, they are more complete than they have ever been before.

3. *Joy improves our relationships.* "I'm convinced," a man pointed out, "that people are attracted to you if you have a positive or joyous frame of mind." He is correct. Think of the people you like to be around. The more positive, the more joyous someone is, the more attractive that person is to us.

Intimate relationships also improve when joyous experiences are shared. For instance, humor, play, and joy are very important to a vital and lasting marriage. A husband told us that he feels joy over "little things" that he shares with his wife. "These are little joys," he said. "We giggle and laugh over inane things. But these joys help bring us together. They solidify our relationship."

In the aftermath of joy, even our relationships with

strangers improve. When a young American vacationing in Jamaica was on her way to a grocery store for some supplies, she noticed a girl in her early teens. "Her flowered dress was faded and torn and several sizes too big for her frail body," she told us. The American felt a twinge of sadness as she entered the store. When she came out, the girl was still there, staring at the woman's new moccasins that she had purchased for the trip. "Pretty," the girl said, pointing at them. The American looked at the girl's bare feet. Impulsively, she took off her shoes and handed them to the girl. The girl began to cry and handed the American a tiny basket she had woven out of grass. The woman described the experience:

"At that moment I experienced joy. It lasted throughout my vacation. While I was there, I had a special feeling of connectedness with the island and the people. And now, whenever I travel, I pay particular attention to the children and try to relate to them."

4. Joy enhances spiritual growth. In his seventeenth-century classic work *The Practice of the Presence of God*, Brother Lawrence pointed out that joy is one of the blessings of sensing God's presence. In other words, spiritual growth produces joy. But the opposite is also true: Joy produces spiritual growth. Joy and spiritual growth nurture and sustain each other.

A middle-aged woman explained the relationship tersely but well: "Joy brings me closer to God. And the closer I get to God, the more joy I feel."

We have discussed the rewards of joy in general terms. In the following chapters, we will discuss the specifics—both the specifics of rewards and specific ways to cultivate joy. The hundreds of Christians who shared their joyous experiences with us talked about many different sources of joy, but five activities—relating, creating, achieving, experiencing, and surrendering—were most frequently mentioned as the context in which joyous experiences occurred. Each of these five activities reflects both the nature of God and a fundamental human need. And each is a way to engage in the joyous celebration of life.

PART II

Cultivating Joy

You show me the path of life.
In your presence there is fullness of joy;
in your right hand are pleasures forevermore.

Psalm 16:11

3

Relating

W e once heard a country preacher relate the parable of the prodigal son in the language of his congregation. He took the congregation through the awful pain the father experienced when the son demanded his portion of the inheritance and left home. He went into detail about the son's misery in the far-off land. And he brought the story to a climax by portraying the father sitting in a rocker on his front porch one evening. He suddenly spied a distant, approaching figure and then jumped to his feet and shouted: "It's my boy! It's my boy!"

The country preacher had captured for his people both the pain and the joy of relating. He had dramatized a truth of the parable that is not often pointed out: Our intimate relationships bring us both agony and exhilaration. Without glossing over the agony, we want to focus on the exhilaration, the joy that is to be found in relating.

Relating Is the Soul of Life

In chapter 1, we noted that each of the five activities associated with joy reflects both the nature of God and a fundamental human need. As far as the nature of God is concerned, the doctrine of the Trinity is an affirmation of relatedness in the essence of God. Jesus taught both his unity with God and his fellowship with the Father: "The Father is in me and I am in the Father" (John 10:38); "I came from the Father and have come into the world; again, I am leaving the world and am going to the Father" (John 16:28). The Holy Spirit is related to both the Son and the Father: "When the Advocate comes, whom I will send to you from the Father, the Spirit of truth who comes from the Father, he will testify on my behalf" (John 15:26).

Our purpose here is not to expound the full doctrine of the Trinity, but only to underscore the point that relatedness is a fundamental attribute of God. Relatedness is also a basic quality of the Christian life. For we have fellowship *(koinonia)* with the Father (1 John 1:3), with Christ (1 Cor. 1:9), with the Holy Spirit (Phil. 2:1), and with each other (Acts 2:42; 1 John 1:7). We will deal with relating to God in a later chapter; here, we want to explore the importance of relating to other people.

The first Christians joyfully banded together in community. They knew the importance of being intimately involved with like-minded others. Paul expressed this hunger for relating in his letter to the Thessalonians: "As for us, brothers and sisters, when, for a short time, we were made orphans by being separated from you—in person, not in heart—we longed with great eagerness to see you face to face. . . . Yes, you are our glory and joy!" (1 Thess. 2:17, 20). It is not surprising, then, that social scientists find relating to be essential to our physical and mental health. It is, in fact, so important to well-being that a therapist friend of ours calls it the "soul of life." He explained:

"When I was a high-school student, I had to read a story called 'The Man Without a Country,' which has stuck in my mind for more than three decades. It was the story of a man who cursed his country and was subsequently sentenced to live apart from his people. He was excised out of his culture. And he lived the rest of his life in despair.

"I've often thought that the same thing happens to people who fail to develop meaningful relationships. They are people who lack more than a country. They are without a soul, because relationships are the soul of life. And like the man without a country, they live with incessant despair."

Relating to others is more than merely the icing on the cake of living. As the story of Adam and Eve reminds us, there is no paradise of nature that can eliminate our need for intimacy: "It is not good that the man should be alone" (Gen. 2:18). We need intimacy from the time we are born. Infants can die if they are deprived of cuddling. Children and adults will suffer various emotional and physical ills if they fail to relate in a meaningful way. One of the most common characteristics of people seeking outpatient psychotherapy is the failure to develop an intimate relationship. It is normal to want intimacy, and it is healthy to relate intimately to others.

Even people who achieve much in life are likely to suffer if they are deficient in relating. Ty Cobb is a baseball legend. Some regard him as the greatest player the game has ever had. He led the American League in batting twelve times, and his lifetime batting average was .367. Looking only at his baseball achievements, we would judge Cobb an enormous success. Unfortunately, there is more to his story.

Cobb died in 1961. The state of Georgia built a museum in his hometown of Royston to honor the man known as the "Georgia Peach." During a financial recession in 1975, the state withdrew its support from the museum. The town council quickly deeded the property to itself and turned the museum into City Hall. Royston still proclaims itself as the "Home of Ty Cobb," but there is little there to commemorate its most famous citizen.

It may be that one of the reasons for the town's neglect was Cobb's personality. He was an intensely competitive man, determined to win at any cost. As a result, he achieved baseball greatness, became a multimillionaire, and made many enemies. But few friends adorned his life. In his later years, he sometimes expressed regret that he had been so driven, so selfish, and so ruthless that he alienated himself from others. He gave generous amounts of money to a number of worthy causes, but his gifts came too late. He died a lonely man, wealthy in achievement and impoverished in relationships.

Relating Is a Major Source of Joy

As the "soul of life," relating is not only a fundamental need but also a major source of joy. Among the people with whom we talked, relating was by far the most common activity cited for producing joy, accounting for nearly half of all the experiences reported to us.

Despite its importance to well-being, there is a tendency to neglect relating for other things. Someone has noted that we have yet to hear anyone on his or her deathbed saying, "I wish I had spent more time at the office." Yet many people, like Ty Cobb, neglect their intimate relationships. The spouse whose absorption in career drains the vitality from the marriage, the parent whose work prevents time with the children, the individual who pursues personal interests at the expense of developing close friendships, the highly ambitious person who competes with and uses people instead of trying to understand, cooperate with, befriend, or help them—all may eventually find themselves with regrets about the course of their lives. Why do they do it?

Recall that all our sources of joy are also sources of pain. Thus, on the one hand, the family is the context for a good deal of trauma. Conflict, frustration, annoyances, and disappointment occur in all families. A serious illness, or the possibility of such an illness in a family member, brings anxiety and pain. Many parents have agonized over a child's spiritual rebellion, drug habit, academic shortcomings, and even the failure to keep a curfew. Many spouses have suffered over suspected indifference or infidelity. Even worse, there is a considerable amount of violent behavior in many families. Family fights are one of the most frequent reasons for police calls.

No question about it. You do take a risk when you establish a family. On the other hand, marriage and children are among the most important sources of gratification in life. In biblical thought, children are a blessing from God. When Elisha wanted to repay the Shunammite woman for her kindness, he promised her that the most serious lack in her life would be remedied—the childless woman would bear a son (2 Kings 4:8-17). The relationship between a husband and a wife is also a source of joy: "Let your fountain be blessed, and rejoice in the wife of your youth" (Prov. 5:18). The relationship between a husband and a wife, Paul wrote, is like that between Christ and his church (Eph. 5:22-32); how could one convey any greater sense of sanctity, richness, and joy to a human relationship than to use such an analogy?

The Two Shall Become One . . . and Rejoice

It may be true, as the philosopher Kierkegaard once wrote, that the marriage ceremony "does not greet the lovers as victors, but invites them to a struggle" (*Edifying Discourses* [New York: Harper & Bros., 1958], p. 183). Nonetheless, for some people both the wedding and the ensuing "struggle" are sources of joy. Colleen, a thirty-four-year-old manager of an art store, speaks with an intensity in her eyes and her voice and has a quick, bright smile as she talks about her wedding:

> "My wedding day was a very special one. I felt joyful the whole day. I felt very special. At the time, I was 23. I had looked forward to getting married all of my life. I felt that God had sent Larry into my life. So my wedding was the culmination of all those years of anticipation."

For Colleen, the marriage itself has been gratifying as well. There have been struggles, of course. She and her husband, Larry, have argued over "petty things" as well as important ones. They agonized when he lost his job and was out of work for three months. They have disagreed about when they should start a family. They have argued about everything from which movie to see to how much time they should spend with his parents. Yet when asked to talk about her experiences of joy, she returns to her marriage:

> "I just enjoy being with Larry. I feel little twinges of joy when we come home at night and see each other. I feel more joy when he does things or says things to let me know that he loves me. I even feel joy when I remember some of the good times we've shared in the past. You know, looking back over our time together, I feel I really came alive with Larry."

One of the interesting things about joy in marriage is that it does not depend on the dramatic event, the breakthrough, or even the unusual. Joy in marriage frequently occurs in the small and everyday occurrences. As one husband expressed it:

"I frequently feel joy with my wife over little things. The other night we were talking about her mother. Now I don't get along too well with my mother-in-law. My wife knows and understands that. She has her own problems with her mother. Anyway, we were talking about me taking her mother to the store, and I meant to say, 'I'll pick her up tomorrow.' But I said, 'I'll trip her up tomorrow.' We both laughed, then my wife hugged me and kissed me. It hit me at that moment what a great relationship we have. And that made me feel joy."

There Is Joy in the Family

Family relations generally are sources of joy for people. Children are one of the most prominent sources. We asked a mother to tell us about joy in her life. She immediately began to share a number of experiences. Then suddenly she stopped. She reflected a moment, and said: "You know, it just struck me that almost all of my experiences of joy have something to do with one or the other of my children."

As in the case of joyous relating with a spouse, an experience of joy with a child can occur in a commonplace event. Some of the everyday kinds of experiences with children in which the people we spoke with found joy were:

- nursing a baby
- laughing with a child
- sharing Christmas or other holidays with children
- times of family togetherness, including family worship and family vacations
- visiting the zoo with a child
- spending time with grandchildren

Such experiences underscore the fact that joy is to be found in everyday events. If joy is elusive, it is because we too often overlook the potential for it in such familiar places. If you fully invest yourself in the experience, you can find joy in sharing the delights and happiness and adventures of children.

You can also find joy in children's achievements or rites of passage. The important thing here is to tune into the joy experienced by the children themselves. Even before they can express themselves, children clearly experience the delight of achievement. We watched an infant tentatively learning to walk one day. He stood up without support. A grin came across his face. He wasn't aware he was being watched. He couldn't yet express his feelings in words. But his grin clearly showed his delight at what he had done.

The possibilities for finding joy in children's achievements or rites of passage are endless. People talked to us about the joy they experienced in such things as:

- an infant who clearly recognized his father for the first time
- a child accepting Christ as Savior, becoming a member of the church, or participating in his or her first communion
- academic achievements of children, from the first days of school to graduation from college
- a child's mastery of, or attempts to master, tasks and challenges
- the marriage of a son or daughter

Of course, children need not be one's own in order to be a source of joy. Again, the joy can be found in some every-day experiences. Dora, a fifty-year-old university professor, told of an experience of joy that occurred when she played Ping-Pong with her three-year-old grandson. The boy was attempting to master a skill that was clearly beyond his capabilities at the time, but the grandmother found his efforts a delight. Laughter punctuated her account:

"He was too short to reach the table. And he couldn't yet hit the ball with the paddle. So he just threw the ball. He would say, 'Ready?' And his eyes would sparkle with anticipation. I would tell him I was all set. Then he'd throw the ball at me with one hand and swing the paddle with the other. I'd get the ball and hit it back. He would watch it go by and then chase it all over the garage. Then he'd come back, grin at me again, and say, 'Ready?'"

Stacy, a thirty-seven-year-old middle-level manager in a food-processing company, has never married or had children of her own. However, when we asked her about a source of joy in her life, she talked about her niece, who gave her "extraordinary joy":

"Since I have no children of my own, I considered her a gift in my life, almost as if she were my own child. When she was an infant, she created a sense of joy just by being here. I love to watch her develop. I can remember when she first started to walk. What a thrill to see her grinning with pride and lurching over toward me as fast as she could go. I love to share Christmas Day with her, to see her excitement throughout the day. Most of all, I just tingle when I see the delight in her eyes when I walk into her home."

Friends Bring Joy

One of the great friendships of the Bible was that between David and Jonathan. After Jonathan's death, David spoke of how rich the friendship had been:

I am distressed for you, my brother Jonathan;
greatly beloved were you to me;
    your love to me was wonderful,
    passing the love of women. (2 Sam. 1:26)

As with family members, the joy experienced in friendships frequently arises in everyday situations when the nature of the relating creates intense emotions. Lisa is thirty-one and single. She is the manager of a large bank. Her "most vivid memory" of joy occurred several years ago on a biking trip with a college friend:

"It happened while my friend Gary was visiting my home following graduation. We had been college friends for three years, and he was as close to me as a brother. It was only a brief visit. One day we went for a bike ride, and after awhile we stopped and sat on some rocks and talked. We talked about our hopes, dreams, fears, and anxieties. We had never talked so intimately before. It made me feel closer than ever to him. Gary and I were good friends, but I never felt that I was a crucial part of his life until we sat there sharing our feelings. He opened himself to me, and I opened myself to him. It was the best time in our relationship. It's hard to describe the moment, but it was truly one of the most joyous days of my life."

In the case of Lisa and Gary, joy was an outgrowth of intimate sharing. Other people talked about joyous experiences with friends in the context of such things as support and trust. In many cases, the joy came out of a time of playfulness or recreation shared with friends. Whatever the situation, friends—like family—are an important source of joy in our lives.

It Is More Blessed to Give

There is another form of relating that is an important source of joy, a form of relating that is expressed in the statement that it is more blessed to give than to receive (Acts 20:35). A number of people we talked with chose an experience of helping someone else as a joyous time for them.

For example, Marian is a thirty-three-year-old recovering alcoholic. Alcoholism cost her two jobs, but now she works successfully as an automobile saleswoman. She also belongs to Alcoholics Anonymous, and it is through her work with that organization that she had a joyous experience: .

"One night I was just about to go to sleep when a woman I work with telephoned. I knew she had a drinking problem, but I was put out that she called me so late. Then she began to share with me some of the painful things in her life. Her troubled marriage. Her problems with her mother-in-law and her kids. As we talked, she got calmer and then she told me that our conversation had helped her understand herself better. She was very grateful to me for being a good listener.

"When I hung up, I got this feeling of overwhelming joy. I was a part of her life, and she trusted me enough to share some very intimate things with me. It made me feel connected to another human being. And through that, I felt connected with the world."

Marian pointed out that helping other people is important to her: "Joy seems to come to me when I'm not wrapped up in myself, when I'm doing things for other people and feel really connected to them by selflessness."

Others made the same point. A minister said that his life had "been blessed with joy, but none so beautiful as when I am giving of myself to others." An executive secretary said that she always tries to help unhappy or troubled people, and that such helping "is my way to get joy. The people I help do the same for me and more." A commercial artist said, "I don't look for joy; it finds me. And it often finds me when I'm doing something for somebody else."

Relating

Why Do Relationships Produce Joy?

A survey of the "self-help" section at your local book-store will quickly reveal the many ways in which relation-ships produce pain in our lives. There are also reasons why they bring joy.

Relationships provide meaning and a sense of being needed. Many people told us that, in part, their joyous experiences with others were rooted in the fact that they were aware they were needed. Lisa said that the joy she felt on her biking trip was the result of the fact that Gary needed and trusted her as a confidante.

Consider the story of thirty-three-year-old Michael:

"My marriage has brought me a lot of joy, but I espe-cially remember one evening when Judy and I came home from work.

"We both have jobs that can be really frustrating at times. Judy likes her work, but her boss can be a real jerk. Anyway, we got home about the same time that evening, and we both looked kind of grim. I asked her how her day was. 'Don't ask,' she told me. Then she asked me how mine was. 'Don't ask,' I told her. We looked at each other and laughed. It was at that moment that I kind of shivered with joy, because I knew that I couldn't make it on my job without some-one like Judy. I really need her. And I knew that she couldn't make it without someone like me. She really needs me. We've talked about it a lot, the way we sup-port each other and need each other. It really hit me that evening because it could have been the bitter end of a rough day. But we turned it into a time of laughing together instead. If coming home to that kind of a rela-tionship can't make you feel joy, nothing can."

Relationships create a climate of love and openness.

One of our favorite stories is about the reticent man who said that he loved his wife so much it was all he could do to keep from telling her about it. Some people find it very hard to openly express their feelings of love. The classic case is illustrated in the exchange: "Do you love me?" "I married you, didn't I?" But joyous experiences are not as likely when people have to infer love from some kind of subtle evidence. We need both the overt expression and the appropriate behavior.

A number of people talked about the joy they experienced when a child, a spouse, or a friend suddenly said, "I love you." To hear and know that you are loved can be exhilarating. However, it is equally invigorating to tell and show someone, "I love you." To *love* as well as to *be* loved, then, is a source of joy. A father of four daughters talked about his love for his family:

> "One of the most joyous experiences I've had occurred a few summers ago when we were vacationing in a cottage on the coast. The family had gathered for breakfast. The girls were talking excitedly about their plans for the day, and my wife was scurrying around the kitchen. Watching them, I was just overwhelmed by an intense feeling of joyful emotion. I loved them so much and was so thankful to the Lord that we had each other. As long as I live, I will never forget that moment!"

Relationships provide understanding and acceptance. To accept another person is to say, in effect, "I understand you and will relate to you in a loving way as you are even though I do not like or approve of all that you are." Such understanding and acceptance provides a context that facilitates joy.

Ben, a twenty-nine-year-old accountant, described an experience of joy when he first met the woman who would eventually become his wife. Without acceptance, their encounter could have quickly gone from high excitement to painful separation:

> "Talk about an adrenaline rush! In the first couple of weeks after I started dating Jackie, I could hardly sleep. I didn't even seem to need it. We spent hours talking together. I had never shared my feelings with anyone like that before. I soon felt that I really understood this woman, and that she really understood me. We accepted each other for what we were. To be honest, there were a couple of things about the other that we each didn't like. We have both worked on these. The main thing is that we could accept each other as we were at the time. We didn't let the few things we didn't like interfere with the many things we liked about each other. We just enjoyed getting to know each other. And for me, the bottom line was joy."

Relationships provide support. A world that is filled with overpowering perils is likely to be a joyless world. One important function of relationships is support, so that the inevitable difficulties of life do not overwhelm us. In other words, we all need to feel some sense of security. We need some back-up protection against the slings and arrows of outrageous fortune.

The support of others, then, opens the way to joyous experiences in an uncertain world. A businesswoman, who is a single mother, described her experience of joy, which occurred at a surprise family party to celebrate her thirtieth birthday. The party was a small one. Only her family—grandmother, mother, father, and four-year-old son—was present. Yet she felt exhilarated. Her exhilaration was rooted in more than the surprise of a party:

The Joy Ride

"Part of the joy for me was what had led up to that day. I thought about all the changes of the past year. I had moved, found a job, and started working on my M.B.A. It was an emotional year. I had a lot of fears and a lot of loneliness. However, my family was consistently supportive and helpful. I knew that they were there, and that they would help me in any way they could. So as I reflected on that, and felt the energy of our love for one another, I experienced tremendous joy. It lasted the whole weekend, and I frequently have flashbacks of that day and my feelings."

Relationships furnish us with a sense of well-being and a generally positive outlook on life. A generally positive attitude does not mean that our friends and family are blind to the darker aspects of human life. However, there is a difference between being aware of such things as pain and suffering and injustice, on the one hand, and viewing all the world through caustic or cynical eyes, on the other hand. In some families, there is nothing right with the world. The government is corrupt, the schools are inept, the media are deceptive, the preacher is mediocre, and Aunt Jane only smiles so much because her rich husband will soon be dead. If there is laughter in such families, it is likely to have a caustic edge to it. There is little joyous laughter and not many joyous experiences.

Joy is fostered by a generally positive outlook. That is, when we believe that there are good people, gratifying opportunities, and hope for the future, we are more likely to experience joy. A positive outlook also includes positive feelings about yourself. Family and friends have a unique ability to provide us with the sense that we are competent and worthwhile. In doing so, they provide the kind of positive context that furnishes the opportunity for us to experience joy.

Building Your Joy Potential

How can you increase the amount of joy in your life? There are many answers, but they all hinge on what we call the Old Faithful principle. Old Faithful is the famous geyser in Yellowstone National Park. The first time we visited the site, we were under the impression that the geyser spewed forth its wonders with almost perfect regularity. We discovered that the eruptions are not that predictable. There is a margin of error in the schedule. While it may be only a matter of minutes, it seems agonizingly long to those waiting for their first view of this natural wonder.

The point is, the eruption *will* occur. The necessary conditions are all present. You can't know the exact time it will take place, but you can be confident that sooner or later you will share in the spectacle. Similarly, you can't manufacture or schedule joy. However, you can create all the conditions necessary for it to erupt. The Old Faithful principle is this: create the conditions, and the joy is sure to occur. In the area of relating, there are a number of ways to build your joy potential.

1. Develop intimate relationships.

Isn't that obvious and unnecessary to say? No, for the emphasis is on *intimate* and not on relationships. Recall the story of Colleen. Before she met Larry, she had a lot of acquaintances and a number of boyfriends. But she lacked intimate relationships:

> "That's why I 'came alive' with Larry. I didn't have anyone with whom I could share my innermost life. I live a long way from my parents. So I mainly talk to them on the telephone. When I was with other people, I either

just listened a lot or I talked about superficial things. From the first, it was easy to open up to Larry. And he opened up to me."

Sharing. Communication. Affection. Colleen found them all with Larry. These are the basic elements of intimacy. You can't be intimate with everyone. Intimacy takes time and energy. And developing intimacy is risky. It means that you make yourself vulnerable. You open up your inner thoughts and feelings for inspection. Yet to shrink away from intimacy, or to neglect it for other concerns, is to excise a major source of joy from your life.

2. Be engaged with the moment.

A father talked about the joy he experienced one night as he read a bedtime story to his seven-year-old daughter:

"We were sitting together on her bed. She was snuggled up against me, resting her head on my shoulder. As I read the story, I was really aware of her closeness and her dependency on me. By the time I had finished the story, her eyelids were drooping and she had snuggled into her pillow. I pulled up the covers, gave her a kiss, then turned out the light. As I looked back at her, I remember thinking about how much I loved her and how much joy she brought into my life."

A key to the father's experience was his complete involvement in the moment. He was not reading in a perfunctory way. It was not a task to simply get through in order to get on to other matters. He was immersed in the moment and focusing on his relationship with his daughter. He had read to his child on many occasions. This night, however, complete involvement in the task became a moment of joy—one which he could have missed if he had viewed the reading as a necessary ritual or had let his mind be distracted by other concerns.

Relating

Remind yourself when you are relating to someone that you want to be immersed in the experience. Practice concentrating on what the other person is saying, feeling, and telling you with his or her nonverbal cues. When you find your mind wandering away or your attention starting to wane, prod yourself to return to a full immersion in the experience. Being engaged with the moment demands effort. The return on your investment, however, is worth it.

3. *Attend to your relationship climate.*

Within your family and among your friends, create conditions that foster joy. Relationships nurture joy by providing feelings of well-being and of being needed, loved, understood, and supported. Certainly, these elements are essential in a healthy relationship climate, a climate that increases the potential for joyous experiences.

One of the major problems in relationships is that too many people get hung up on "shoulds." For example: "I work hard at being a loyal friend; my friend *should* acknowledge my efforts and never criticize me." Or: "I am doing my best to be a decent individual and maintain a good home; my children *should* respect that and follow my rules and not cause problems." Or as an executive put it: "I work hard. I keep my nose clean. I'm a good citizen. I expect my family to do the same."

Unfortunately, being a good citizen and a hard, honest worker won't ensure healthy relationships. You can't take family or friends for granted. You have to attend to the climate of your relationships as diligently as you attend to other matters in life. Indeed, healthy relating involves some work. However, the payoff will be a quantum leap in joy potential.

4. *Increase your empathy quotient.*

Most people would like to have a high I.Q. We admire people who are exceptionally intelligent. For purposes of joy, however, it is more important to have a high E.Q., or empathy quotient. Joy is an equal opportunity experience for people of varying amounts of intelligence. It is not, however, equally likely for people with varying amounts of empathy. Joy in relating often comes when two people share an experience and each understands how the other feels about it. The man who said he would "trip up" his mother-in-law had a joyous experience because he and his wife understood each other's reactions to the statement.

Empathy is a godly quality. God has perfect empathy, for he "searches every mind, and understands every plan and thought" (1 Chron. 28:9). As "imitators of God" (Eph. 5:1), we need to develop our capacity for empathy, which, like engagement with the moment, can be learned and increased. Again, it requires conscious effort and practice. It is the kind of thing you can practice in an intimate relationship. By carefully observing and listening, try to "read" your friend or family member. Then tell the person what you think he or she is feeling and experiencing. Over time, you should become increasingly accurate, which means that you are raising your E.Q.

5. Reserve a part of your life for helping others.

Many people help others indirectly, by tithing or giving money to a particular cause. Such indirect help is important, and it brings considerable satisfaction. But to increase your joy potential, you need to reserve a part of your life for giving direct as well as indirect help.

Ralph is the busy owner of an architectural landscape firm. He has always helped others indirectly through gifts of money. One day he discovered that he could still take a piece of his busy life and set it aside for some direct help as well. He learned that it was possible to find joy when he battled against his own weary reluctance and committed himself to direct involvement.

Ralph learned all this when a friend asked him to spend the night at their church with some homeless men. Ralph agreed with reluctance. For three hours before going to sleep, he talked with a man who was embarrassed to be there:

> "We talked about the breakup of his marriage, how he quit work afterward because he was too depressed to go in, and how he hoped to get his life back together. The next morning, he grasped my hand and thanked me for helping him. Helping him! He still had no home, no job, and no family. But he seemed to have new hope in his eyes. And I went home to my wife feeling higher than I had for years. The joy was so intense, that I have been giving a night a week ever since."

As Ralph discovered, you don't have to give all of your life to helping others in order to have joy. The great majority of us will never be a Mother Teresa, but we can still experience the joy of helping others by reserving a *part* of our lives for serving others. Even if it is only a few hours a month, directly helping people enormously raises your joy potential.

Creating

A sixty-year-old professional told us that he remembers very little about his early school years. However, one incident is embedded in his memory. When he was in second grade, he made a drawing that his teacher praised highly and hung on the wall for the other pupils to admire. "It was the first time I recall," he said, "feeling the thrill of doing something creative."

He is grateful that he learned at an early age to think of himself as a creative person. Ever since, he has striven to experience again and again the joy of being creative. Indeed, those who create find it to be one of the more joyous activities of their lives.

To Create Is to Imitate God

To start at the beginning, "God created the heavens and the earth" (Gen. 1:1). In the end, God will create a new heaven and a new earth (Rev. 21:1). In the meantime, we can rejoice at all the creative works of God: "For you, O Lord, have made me glad by your work; at the works of your hands I sing for joy" (Ps. 92:4).

Creating is part of the nature of God. When we ask, "Who is God?" at least part of the answer has to be that

God is he who creates. Note that we said *creates* and not just *created.* For God's creative activity continues in us. A Christian is "a new creation; everything old has passed away; see, everything has become new!" (2 Cor. 5:17). And God "is at work in you, enabling you both to will and to work for his good pleasure" (Phil. 2:13). We were created in the image of God, the Creator. We, therefore, have a need to imitate God in being creative.

Noted psychotherapist Rollo May argued that we are driven by a need to relate to others such that we cultivate, procreate, and help fashion the world in which we live. In other words, we have a need to be creative. Abraham Maslow, the pioneer of the psychology of self-actualization, found creativity to be one of the characteristics of people who were realizing their full potential—the goal of self-actualization. Maslow also pointed out that creativity involves more than a product. People can be creative at anything from their sense of humor to housekeeping to teaching to problem solving.

When you act or think creatively, you imitate God, the Creator. You fulfill one of your fundamental needs, and you open yourself to the experience of joy. Your creative activity may not be dramatic—may not lead to recognition—but it most likely will bring you joy.

To Create Is to Rejoice

Kenneth is a thirty-five-year-old counselor whose avocation is music. When asked about an experience of joy, he reached back in his memory to when he got his first piano at age thirteen. He also had a small chord organ, which he moved close to the piano so that he could play chords on the organ with one hand while playing the melody on the piano with the other.

One day it struck him that he could try to duplicate the chords on the piano. He worked by trial and error, listening carefully to the organ chords and then matching the notes on the piano. It took a number of frustrating weeks, but the frustrations eventually yielded to monumental joy:

"I had discovered chord theory! I learned the concept of chords, how to play them, and the great sound I could get from playing them. A whole new world of possibilities opened to me. And for the first time, I realized my creative potential. At the outset I thought no one else knew what I had discovered, and I wanted to share my insights with everyone. When I found out that others already knew, it didn't dim my joy—I had discovered it on my own. Besides, part of the joy was that I knew I would be creative for the rest of my life."

Kenneth's experience underscores two important points. First, creative activity tends to produce joy. And second, creative activity is not limited to great artists, writers, and scientists. One mistake that some people make is to think of creativity as the province of the few who are endowed with this special capacity. However, everyone has the potential for creative efforts. No one is creative at everything, but everyone is creative—at least, potentially so—at something. The dictionary defines *creativity* as originality of thought or action or expression. Whenever you do something or think about something that is innovative for *you,* you are being creative—even if someone else has done the same thing.

Newton and Leibniz discovered calculus independently of each other. Both are rightly regarded, therefore, as creative men. There are many other examples of simultaneous and independent innovation in the history of science. In each case, the innovation was original to each individual and was, therefore, creative activity. To be creative does not mean that you have to do something unique in the world's history; it means only that you have to think or do something original to you. All of us have that capacity.

Why is creative activity likely to produce joy? There are a number of reasons.

First, creativity is its own reward. Because creating is imitating God, and because creating is a basic need, we are likely to experience joy in the very act of being creative. That is, your creative efforts don't have to lead to something productive or successful in order to bring joy.

One man told us how a creative idea that failed gave him joy. The idea was a new business venture—manufacturing a somewhat innovative and inexpensive product for automobiles. He discussed the idea with a friend, who was interested in working with him to develop it:

> "For three weeks, I spent every spare moment I had researching the idea, looking into ways to finance the start up of the business, and getting information about the mechanics of setting up a business in my area. I felt a sense of joy the whole time. It was really exhilarating. Then we hit a snag in the form of patents. Our business never got off the ground. But I have no regrets. It was a creative idea, and I still have good feelings about it."

Second, creative activity builds self-esteem. Marilyn is a writer of children's stories. She didn't begin publishing them until she was in her forties. Although she wrote her first story when she was about nine years old and continued to write during her teen years, she had no idea that her work was publishable. "The stories got nothing more than a ho-hum response from my parents and my teachers. No encouragement whatsoever."

Fortunately, Marilyn didn't throw out her stories. For thirty years they stayed with her. While cleaning out the attic, she came across them again:

"There was no name or date on the first couple, so I thought they might have been written by my niece or nephew. Then I saw my name and realized that these were all my old stories. I experienced a great rush of joy. And part of the joy was in the realization that I had found the stories to be quite good before I even realized they were mine. After that, I started writing again. I knew I had the talent for it, and nothing was going to deter me."

With her self-confidence enormously boosted by the joyous discovery of her creative potential, Marilyn embarked on a new phase of her life.

Third, creative activity is a "eureka" experience. Eureka means "I have found it." We all know the exhilaration that comes when we have done something that elicits a "eureka!" In the case of creative activity, it may be a sense of "I have found it" or "I have done it." It may be a creative solution to a problem or a creative way to do a task or a creative method of childrearing.

A young mother was perplexed by her three-year-old son's habit of coming into her bed in the middle of the night and disturbing his parents' sleep. Nothing she said seemed to make any difference. Her son was not convinced by his mother's argument that he would be more comfortable in his own bed.

Her son's fourth birthday was approaching, so one day she tried something different. She began telling him: "When you're four, you won't come into our bed at night anymore. Big boys sleep in their own beds." She repeated this message frequently the week before his birthday. It worked! She felt joy at having solved the problem in a creative way. Moreover, she experienced the joy again when she shared her idea with a friend who had a similar problem and later found that the method worked for her as well.

The Joy of Creating Life

God's primary desire is to create life. In the beginning, it was not sufficient to create masses of inorganic matter; rather, God willed life in his universe. God created various forms of life—plants, animals, and humans—and God continues this life-creating activity by nurturing us and fashioning us so that we not only have life, but "have it abundantly" (John 10:10). These two ways of creating life—bringing life into existence and enriching and enhancing life that exists—are joyous activities. We will look first at the joy of bringing life into the world.

Creating human life is joyous for both men and women. In fact, we found that men are as likely as women to identify the birth of a baby as an experience of joy. Some fathers said that the birth of each of their children was a time of great joy. Russ, a thirty-five-year-old automobile dealer, put it this way:

"I think the biggest experiences of joy I have ever had were the births of my two children. I was twenty-six and twenty-eight when they were born. I was in the delivery room with my wife both times. When the kid comes out, something—and I don't know what it is—comes over you. Maybe it's the thought that the child is a part of you. You helped create it. I was so joyful, I wanted to cry. In fact, I did cry."

Similarly, Gary, a forty-year-old small business owner, told us how he and his wife were both "scared to death" to have children because of the tenuous nature of the business he had started. After debating and arguing about it, they agreed to "go for broke." His business was consuming, but Gary attended the Lamaze classes faithfully with his wife. He felt joyous as he watched his wife grow larger. "I can remember kissing her abdomen and singing to our baby at night," he recalled. He described the birth of their son this way:

> "It was an extraordinary experience, really intense. My son was so beautiful. He was perfect. A miracle. They had to finally kick me out of the hospital that night. I would have stayed all night if they had let me. The adrenalin rush lasted for five days. I guess it was the 'highest' time of my entire life."

Not all fathers speak in such ecstatic terms. Some men become fathers with relatively little interest. The less involved a father is in the pregnancy, the less is his joy at childbirth. It is the involved father who is the joyous father.

And what about mothers? Someone has said that giving birth to a child is like taking your lower lip and pulling it up over your head. Nevertheless, about one out of seven women in our survey named the birth of a child as a peak experience of joy. The joy is not likely to come in the delivery process, but in the aftermath. Crystal, a twenty-eight-year-old nurse, told us about the birth of her first child:

> "I felt an overwhelming sense of joy. I don't think it was actually giving birth that did it, but holding my baby afterward. My own little creation. Whatever it was, I know that I felt on top of the world when I held my daughter."

Crystal's joy was intensified by the fact that the birth of her daughter was the first significant, creative act of her life. Her parents had divorced when she was a girl, and she had a difficult relationship with her stepfather. As a result, many of her early years were ones in which she concentrated on "just hanging in there." It was in childbirth that she discovered her own power to be creative, to focus on something more than mere survival, to participate with God in bringing life into the world.

Not only parents rejoice in new life. A number of grandparents told us that they felt more joy at the births of their grandchildren than even of their own children. Uncles and aunts spoke of the joy they felt when a new baby arrived in the family. And one nurse said that the first time she saw a birth in the delivery room she was moved by "tears of joy at the miracle of birth."

What is it about the birth experience that brings joy? Is it the moment of arrival that brings joy? Is it, as Crystal indicated, holding the baby for the first time? Or does the joy begin earlier? Actually, both men and women indicated feelings of joy at every stage of the birth experience, exulting in the thought of bringing life into the world. Many men talked to us about the joy they experienced while watching their wives' changing bodies and anticipating the arrival of the life taking shape therein.

Like Russ, many men also told about laughing or crying or both when they watched their children being born. One new father said, "I had a lump in my throat that would not go away for a while. I was just speechless. I couldn't even verbalize the intense feeling of happiness that I had. It was just a total experience, all-encompassing."

Although few women defined pregnancy itself as a time of joy, some told us they experienced joy when they found out they were pregnant. A librarian told how she felt joy when she first heard the baby's heartbeat: "I was, at that moment, full of life, love, and a sense of connectedness with my baby."

Most mothers talked about the joy they felt when they saw or held the baby for the first time. They described the experience as a sense of increased spirituality, peace, relief, personal accomplishment and completion, pride, creativity, bonding, love, and joy.

The Joy Ride

The Joy of Enhancing Someone Else's Life

As we noted earlier, it is also creative activity in a biblical sense when you enhance someone's life in a way that enables that person to live more abundantly. Such creative work is joyous activity as well.

Some people have numerous opportunities to enhance the lives of others through their careers or work situations. The joy, however, comes when there is some response from the recipients. When that happens, both the joy and the life-enhancement are likely to be mutual. For example, a man who works as an aide in a psychiatric hospital said:

"Just last week, I was working with a teenage patient, and he told me that he was glad I would be at his graduation ceremony at the hospital. His face glowed with happiness. And I felt joy at the thought that I had helped him reach that point."

Similarly, a pastor said that one of the more joyous days of his ministry occurred when a young man came up to him after a worship service and said: "I have a gift for you." The young man stood with his wet-eyed wife and told about his twenty-year alienation from his father. "I want you to know," the young man said, "that your sermon today has given me the courage to go to my father and seek reconciliation."

You don't have to be a nurse or a minister to have opportunities to enhance the lives of others. Some people find opportunities in volunteer work. Marsha, a nineteen-year-old student, offered to help her pastor teach the annual confirmation class at her church. "I was high as a kite," she said, "when I looked at their faces on Confirmation day. And they all looked at me with such love and gratitude. What an experience!" Nine months later, she said she still recaptures some of the joy when she reflects on the fact that she had an impact on young lives.

We all will have opportunities in some way or other if we want them. In a church discussion group, someone said we need to pray for opportunities to serve. Someone else commented that we need to pray to take advantage of the opportunities we have. But perhaps what we really need is to pray for the grace to be the kind of people God can use to facilitate the work that he is doing in those we encounter from day to day.

Nan is a white-haired, serene-looking woman who strives to be Christian in all her dealings. A joyous experience she remembers well occurred nearly two decades ago when a well-dressed man appeared at her door. She recognized him immediately, but for a moment she was speechless. Then she invited him in for a cup of tea and a visit. This was the second time that the man had appeared unexpectedly at her door.

The first time had occurred a year earlier when the man stood at her door, looking like a tramp. He asked her if she had any work he could do. She told us that although she didn't have any work for him, "he looked so harmless and so weary that I invited him in for a sandwich and a cup of tea." They talked together, and the man admitted that he had been in prison for arson. While he was imprisoned, his family had deserted him. When he was released, he was unable to find work.

After thanking her for the meal, he left. She heard nothing more from him until he appeared a year later looking like a prosperous businessman instead of a down-and-out tramp. He told her that nearly everyone he had met after his release from prison had treated him with either fear or contempt or both. He had felt completely defeated. But Nan had changed that:

The Joy Ride

"It seems that I had said one thing that made a difference. I called him 'sir.' No one had said 'sir' to him in years. He said it had restored his sense of dignity. He left the house with a new spirit and a new determination to do something with his life."

It was a joyous moment for Nan when the man told her of the impact she had on him. "I almost feel like I've had another child," she said. "I gave a man life, and I didn't even know what I was doing." In another sense, however, Nan did know what she was doing. She was acting in a Christian manner toward another person. The result was the creation of a new life for the man, and a joyous experience for Nan, who said that the incident has made all subsequent efforts to enhance the lives of others more pleasurable. She always reminds herself that she could be helping to change someone's life.

Building Your Joy Potential

Like the professional man with whom we began this chapter, you can cultivate opportunities to experience joy in the area of creativity. As a result of his childhood experience, he has been an avid proponent of the joys of creative efforts. "Whenever someone tells me they wish they could do something," he says, "I immediately encourage them not to assume they can't and to give it a try." Knowing how joyous it is to be creative, he urges others to realize that they, too, have creative potential. And that's the first step in building your joy potential.

1. Affirm your creative potential.

By this time you are convinced, we hope, that you are, or can be, creative in something. Keep in mind that there are numerous realms of life in which you can be creative.

Creating

Unfortunately, the very word *creativity* is likely to bring to mind such names as Da Vinci or Edison or Einstein. Yet you need neither to be notable nor gain notoriety in order to be creative.

Fred, a forty-five-year-old draftsman, is creative. "I had an idea some years ago for a new mechanical device," he told us. In his imagination he constructed a model, and then he went to work and built it. He anxiously waited to see if it would work as he had conceived it in his mind, and it did. He described, "I was filled with joy. The feeling was almost spiritual. Something I had only dreamed about was a reality. It had come from inside of me, and it worked, and I was thrilled."

And then what? Did it lead to a patent? Did Fred gain a reputation of being a modern Edison? Did his creation bring him fame and wealth? The answers are no, no, and no. It doesn't matter. Being creative brought him joy.

To affirm your creative potential means to accept the fact that you have the potential and, like Fred, to put it into action. But wait! you say. How can I put my creative potential into action when I'm not even certain about the ways in which I can be creative? That leads to the second step.

2. Discover your creative potential by exploring.

Many people assume in advance that they have no creative ability in certain areas. That's a mistake. We urge you to explore whatever interests you.

Paula, a retired secretary, has painted for her family and friends for many years. Her paintings give her joy. She was in her thirties, however, before she ever tried to paint. One day, while shopping with a friend, she noticed in a store window a painting that she particularly liked. "I wish I could do that," she told her friend. They had often spent time browsing in art stores, but it was the first time Paula had expressed such a desire. Her friend looked at her for a moment, then said, "What makes you think you can't?"

Paula laughed and thought no more about it. On her next birthday, however, she received a surprise present from her friend—a set of paints and brushes. Paula's friend had forced her to explore an activity that she might never have pursued on her own. Since she didn't know how to proceed, Paula went to the library and checked out a book on oil painting. Three weeks later, she proudly showed her first creation to her friend.

Another area to explore for creative activity is one in which you are having a problem. It may be a childrearing concern, like the mother who wanted to keep her son from coming into her bed at night. It may be a relationship at work, or a task that you find onerous, or a financial situation that perplexes you. In essence, the way to be creative is to ask such questions as: How else could I handle this? What other way could this be done? What other options do I have in this situation?

Any kind of problem situation is an opportunity for a creative response. For instance, consider the response of Ted to a situation that could have resulted in an utterly miserable family vacation. Ted and his wife, who own a small flower shop, take their two children on a cross-country camping trip each year. A few years ago, they decided to choose the back roads and see more of the "real" country. They were in Kansas looking for a campground, but there were none to be found. They stopped in a small town and asked a man for advice. He led them to a free camp area provided by the town. They were the only people there.

As they set up their tent, they noticed the black clouds filling the sky. Shortly after going to bed, a horrendous storm swept over the area. Ted's wife and children ran to the car and tried to sleep there amid various toys and travel equipment. Ted decided to stay in the tent. The rain continued all night, and no one slept very well. Tired and irritable, the family began loading up the car with their soggy gear at dawn. Ted was feeling extremely grumpy. Then he had a creative inspiration:

"I was suddenly struck with the absurdity of these kinds of events making us negative and grouchy, as though God had sent the storm to ruin our vacation. I felt myself becoming serene. Then I felt a kind of elation as I realized that I had control of my emotions and that I could save this day or ruin it by my attitude. I could rant and rave to no avail, or I could do something else."

The "something else" at first startled his family. Ted decided to "abandon" himself "to the childish joys of a small boy puddle-jumping." He shed all his inhibitions:

"With total abandon, I lost myself in the experience. I danced a jig around a puddle and began whooping it up in the rain. After a puzzled look and a pause, my wife joined me. The kids looked at us in disbelief, but then looked relieved, and soon we were all in the puddles. We were more soaked than we had been for the past twelve hours. But we were all joyful. Four wet people piled into a wet car and happily headed off in search of breakfast."

As Ted's experience illustrates, we *always* have options. And that means we always have the opportunity to be creative.

3. *Be willing to take risks.*

Creative people know that they will not succeed every time. One reason that some people do not exercise their creative ability is their fear of failure. In order to realize your creative potential, then, you must accept the risk of failure. Paula could have discovered that she had no talent for painting. It was a risk she had to take in order to discover how creative she actually is.

There are other risks. When thirty-seven-year-old Jacqueline got pregnant, she faced the risks of severe financial problems and unmanageable disruption in her life. She and her husband lived in different places at the time because of their jobs. To say the least, they weren't pleased about the pregnancy. Jacqueline tells this story:

"In the midst of our unhappiness, something seemed to tell me that this child had to be born because it was special. And the feeling remained strong throughout the pregnancy. I never doubted that I had made the right decision.

"Then, when our daughter was born, when I saw her for the first time, it was a true spiritual experience for me. A mixture of peacefulness, contentment, joy—oh, yes, great joy! I remember saying to myself, 'This is what we were supposed to do. This is what life is really about. Now we are complete.' "

Jacqueline and her husband took the risks, created life, and rejoiced.

This is not to say that you easily dismiss the risks. In some cases, the risks may be too great. We were urged by a skydiving enthusiast to take up the sport. He promised us that it would be exhilarating and liberating—"like nothing else you've ever done." Skydiving could prove a creative and joyous experience for us. But we'll never know. The risks are unacceptable as far as we're concerned. By the same token, there are nearly always some risks involved in striving to be creative. Accept the risks, and know the joy of imitating God by creating.

Achieving

C an you imagine a joyous experience that centers on Kool-Aid? It happened to Nancy, a Midwestern housewife when she was six years old. At the time, her father was a Marine. Their family of six struggled each month to keep enough food in the house. Nancy recalls that they were on their last package of Kool-Aid, waiting for their end-of-the-month check to arrive. Once the check came, her mother would go to the grocery store.

That evening, they were having hamburgers and Kool-Aid for dinner. It was Nancy's turn to mix the Kool-Aid in the gallon glass jar that would be filled to the brim. Since she was only six, she had to stand on a chair and mix it in the sink:

> "As I was lifting the Kool-Aid out of the sink, the chair started to wobble. I lost my footing, and my mother and brother and two sisters watched in horror as I held that pitcher up, trying to catch my balance. I slipped and rolled to the floor, but I never spilled a drop! It was like a miracle. I was overjoyed. I hadn't let my family down. I saved our precious drink. I was a hero."

The incident is vivid in her mind some thirty years later because it bolstered her sense of being able to achieve something difficult. Achieving, like relating and creating, is an important source of joy.

You Need to Achieve

When leading the Israelites to the promised land, Moses summoned them together and reminded them of the mighty acts of God that had delivered them: "For it is your own eyes that have seen every great deed that the LORD did" (Deut. 11:7). This is one of the great insights of the Old Testament: Our God is a God who acts, who achieves things in human lives. God is not removed from human affairs; rather, he continues to act in our lives. As Paul affirmed: "I am confident of this, that the one who began a good work in you will bring it to completion by the day of Jesus Christ" (Phil. 1:6).

We, who serve a God who achieves, also need to achieve. One way to achieve is through personal accomplishments of various kinds. Another way is through work. Love and work, Freud once observed, are the two major ingredients in emotional well-being (*Civilization and Its Discontents* [New York: W. W. Norton, 1963]). People who are satisfied with their work tend to be more satisfied with life in general. People who achieve at work tend to feel better about themselves. That's why the teacher could say: "So I saw that there is nothing better than that all should enjoy their work" (Eccles. 3:22). And that's why John could write: "I have no greater joy than this, to hear that my children are walking in the truth" (3 John 4). John's "children" were the fruit of his work as an apostle; effective work produced joy for him.

Some philosophers have noted that it is the struggle, the striving for something, not the actual achievement that pleases us. It is true that we need to be challenged regularly, and it is true that completion of something may bring a sense of loss or sadness. Yet it is also true that struggle without achievement degenerates to frustration, anger, or despair.

Even if there is no sense of joy at the time you complete something, the joy may come as you reflect on what you have achieved. A young man who completed a three-and-a-half-week survival expedition in the desert felt only relief and gratitude initially, but later his feelings changed. He explained:

> "In the aftermath, as I thought about what I had done, I had a growing sense of joy. I had conquered that bleak terrain. I had not allowed the desolate environment to overcome me. At times, I desperately wanted to quit, but I didn't. And when I thought about all that, I rejoiced."

If you sometimes get weary of the obstacles to achievement, keep in mind that it is precisely those obstacles that make the final victory so joyous. Would the young man have rejoiced if the expedition had been something anyone could easily do? When Jesus sent seventy of his disciples out on a mission, they "returned with joy, saying, 'Lord, in your name even the demons submit to us!'" (Luke 10:17). To overcome demonic obstacles was a far more joyous experience than to gain an easy, effortless victory. Keeping in mind, then, that there are likely to be obstacles in any effort to achieve something, let us look at the various ways in which achieving can lead to joy.

Achieve a New Beginning

We tend to think of achieving in terms of the end of something, but achieving can also occur at the beginning of something, particularly when it means either that you take some risks in order to begin or that the beginning represents the fulfillment of a dream. A young man told us that one of his most memorable experiences of joy was when he quit his job as a bank teller in order to resume work on a college degree. He had attended school for two years, dropped out, and worked at the bank for the next five years. It was a risky decision for him, because he wasn't sure how he would support himself. But he still felt joy, knowing he was entering a new phase of his life:

> "I quit a boring job at the bank. I knew that if I didn't finish my education I would be working there for thirty years, and I didn't want that. I want a career in the biological sciences. I think that will be a lot more satisfying. I really want to excel at something, and I think this will give me that chance."

A new beginning, then, is anything that alters the course of your life. The alteration may or may not be something dramatic. It could be a return to school, a change of career, a decision to marry, a commitment to master a new skill, or an effort to change your attitude or personality. The joy comes from opening a new door and anticipating the new opportunities for growth and fulfillment.

Patricia, a young businesswoman, illustrates the other way a new beginning can be joyous—as the fulfillment of a dream. In Patricia's case, it was a four-year dream. Shortly after graduating from college and starting to work for a corporation, she began to dream of her own business. Four years of thinking and planning finally led to the establishment of the business. She recalled:

> "It went from my mind to actuality. I stood outside and watched when the men came to put up the sign. I stared at that sign for thirty minutes, and tears just kept streaming from my eyes. It had been on paper for so long. Now it was real."

The Joy Ride

Patricia also risked a good deal, of course. She gave up her job with the corporation and entered the perilous world of small business. Three years later, her business is thriving. But the highest point of her joy came at the beginning when she realized the fulfillment of her dream.

Master a New Skill

A second way to experience the joy of achieving is to master a new skill. The skill can be largely intellectual, such as learning a new language; or it can be physical, such as learning to swim; or it can combine physical and intellectual skills, such as learning to use a computer.

Have you seen the triumphant look on the face of a small child who masters a new skill? You may be able to recall having that experience when you were a child. Twenty-six-year-old Kristin told us about the joyous experience that she had at age seven when she learned to ride a bicycle. It was particularly enjoyable because of her two older brothers, who both knew how to ride and had teased her:

"They thought they were hot stuff, and better than me because I was little and a girl. I was worried that I'd never be able to do it without training wheels. But it finally all came together, and it was like magic. I was a queen that day. My parents practically had to drag me off the bike. I can still remember how I felt—like the world was mine for the taking."

Clearly, Kristin's achievement enhanced her sense of her own abilities. One of the benefits of mastering a new skill is that it makes you feel better about yourself. Some Christians have a problem with that notion, thinking that we need to demean ourselves or engage in spiritual self-flagellation. But we are speaking about feeling good about yourself in the context of who you are—one redeemed by, and empowered by, Jesus Christ. As with Paul, you can rejoice as you affirm: "I can do all things through him who strengthens me" (Phil. 4:13).

Some people find special joy in mastering a skill for which they seem ill-fitted. Again, it is the overcoming of a particularly difficult obstacle that intensifies the joy.

Tammy, a thirty-one-year-old occupational therapist, suffered from asthma and a variety of allergies as a child and was unable to participate with others in sports and other outdoor activities. As a teenager, she outgrew her allergies but developed knee muscle problems. By the time she entered college, she had virtually no experience in contact sports. Friends would neither expect nor ask her to participate in such activities. She was understandably overjoyed the day she won a black belt in karate.

How did it happen? While in college, she became interested in self-defense after reading about a number of assaults on women on campus. Tammy felt safe as long as she was with her boyfriend, but he worked nights and could not pick her up after her evening classes. So she enrolled in a martial arts course. She enjoyed it greatly. After graduation and marriage, she continued her training in a private studio in her town. She recalled the day when she was ready to test for her black belt:

"My husband and I, together with some friends, drove to the city the night before and stayed in a motel. I was bounding with energy and singing to myself most of the night as we walked the boulevards to control my restlessness.

"The test itself lasted about twenty-five minutes in front of a panel of ten black belts. I was so focused that I was totally unaware of the audience. I barely heard the chairman's request for certain forms, kicks, and strikes. But when they announced that I passed, I let out a big whoop of joy and hugged my husband and friends. The satisfaction was incredible."

Tammy is using her skill to teach a class in self-defense for women. After years of struggling with physical disabilities, her achievement has led her, in her words, to keep "looking over to the next rainbow and its pot of gold." The joy of achieving gave birth to the expectation of additional conquests.

You also can find joy in mastering a new skill that enables you to expand your range of emotional experience. For example, some people are emotionally handicapped because they have never learned to acknowledge and express anger in a healthy way. Forgetting that God expresses anger, that Jesus got angry, and that Paul specifically tells us to express our anger (Eph. 4:26), they repress their anger as something inappropriate for Christians. Learning to express your anger in an appropriate Christian way can be a liberating, indeed a joyous, experience.

Other emotions can be similarly suppressed for a variety of reasons. It took Carl, who is now forty, the first twenty-seven years of his life to learn how to cry. He felt that "real men" simply do not cry. He said, "I felt that crying was a form of weakness, including a weakness in my faith." A dog caused him to cry his first tears as an adult, and it was a joyous experience.

The dog's name was Zack. Carl got Zack after he moved from California to Michigan to attend school. His loneliness was intensified by the paucity of sunshine and the cold winter. At Christmas, he decided to adopt a pet. He found Zack, a multicolored fox terrier, at the Humane Society. For the next two years, Carl and Zack provided each other with companionship and fun. "When Zack looked at me," Carl said, "his tail wagged and his body swayed from side to side. I felt like I was watching love in action."

Achieving

After two years, Carl was admitted to a university in Chicago to pursue graduate work. Unfortunately, he couldn't take Zack along because the dorm where he was to live did not permit dogs. So he returned Zack to the Humane Society. Carl described how he felt: "I was broken-hearted. I walked away from that building with both pain and guilt. How could I explain to Zack why he couldn't be with me anymore? What could I say to someone who had seemed to love me so freely and unconditionally?"

That was not the moment that Carl cried, however. It happened in Chicago. He was lying on the floor of his dorm room one evening when he suddenly remembered the times on the floor with Zack in Michigan:

"Zack was different when I was on the floor. He was all over me, like he reveled in me coming down to his level. It was as if he could share more of himself with me. We both had a ball, rolling around and wrestling. And as I thought about it, I just suddenly burst into tears. I cried a long time. And when I stopped, I felt free. Freer than I had ever felt in my life."

In those moments of feeling free, Carl rejoiced. It was the joy of discovering a new facet of himself, and the joy of being able to express freely his feelings. It was the joy of being released into a wider range of experience. Paradoxical as it may sound, that experience of grief became for him "the joy of joys" because it broke open for him a new dimension of life. Carl has mastered the skill of emotional expression; he is no longer afraid to experience or to express any human emotion.

Reach a Personal Best

When we say "master" a new skill, that doesn't mean that you will always be a peak performer in that skill. Few people ever master a skill in the sense that they accomplish the ultimate in that skill. Once you have developed a skill, therefore, you can find further joy in improving your performance.

Obviously, we are not talking about something like making the *Guinness Book of World Records* for crying. But think of the other cases we discussed. Kristin could have set a goal of riding her bike a particular distance or of racing. Tammy could have stopped far short of the black belt and still felt joy over achieving skill in karate.

A "personal best" does not mean a world record, and we would not recommend that you set such a high standard for yourself. Your personal best could be like that of the young man who studied piano for a number of years and felt joy when he was able to play well a relatively simple composition of Chopin. "It was my first classical piece," he said, "but I was ecstatic as I sat there and was finally able to play it through flawlessly."

Your "personal best" also does not mean that you have reached the limit of your ability. The young man went on to master more difficult pieces on the piano; each new conquest brought him a new experience of joy. Since few if any of us reach the ultimate of what can be done with a particular skill, the possibilities for continuing experiences of joy are endless.

Vera took up running when she became a grandmother. "I love being a grandmother," she said, "but I don't want to look like one." Running seemed to be the best way to keep her body trim. The first year, she ran one mile three times a week. The second year, she ran four miles four times a week. The third year, she ran six times a week. One day that year she ran sixteen miles. She said:

"I felt great joy at each of these milestones in my running. Each time I thought I had reached my limit, but each time I took that as a challenge and tried to do more. For a time, I believed I could never go beyond ten miles. So when I reached sixteen on that April day, I felt like a real athlete. And I felt extreme joy. In fact, running and joy are inseparable for me."

Note that at one year, Vera's personal best was one mile, and that brought her joy. The point is that when you strive for a personal best, don't measure your performance against anything except yourself. It didn't matter to Vera that millions of people could run more than a mile. She had never run before. A mile for her was a personal best and, therefore, a cause for joy.

Strive for Excellence at Work

Americans tend to have ambivalent feelings about work. On the one hand, there's the "thank God it's Friday" attitude that views work as a burden from which the weekend offers liberation. On the other hand, surveys report that the great majority of us say we would continue to work even if we had enough, or won enough, money to retire. Perhaps when we acknowledge that we would want to continue working, we are at least dimly aware that work is a potential source of joy to us. And if we strive for excellence in our work, it can be an actual source of joy.

The joy can come in a couple of ways. One way, of course, is through recognition of your achievement. In Jesus' parable of the talents, the master said "well done" to the two men who had used their talents to earn more, and completed his appreciation by saying "enter into the joy of your master" (Matt. 25:21, 23). Thus did our Lord link the recognition of excellence to joy.

Rita, an office manager in her thirties, had one of the more joyous experiences of her life when she was twenty-five. She was working in the offices of a fast-food corporation. Her boss was promoted and was asked to recommend a replacement. She recalled the experience:

> "I remember when my boss called me in and told me I was just right for the job even though I had only been with the corporation a few months. My boss said he really appreciated my high-quality performance and commitment to the business. I was excited. I was nervous. And I was overjoyed that they felt I was capable of moving to a higher position."

Office workers told us about the joy they experienced when they won some kind of employee award. Teachers told us about the joy of former students returning to say thank you. Counselors told us about the joy of helping people or bringing couples back together, and the intensifying of that joy when the clients offered gratitude for the help they received.

Even if there is no recognition, however, striving for excellence can still bring joy simply because of its inherent value. Many of our parents tried to teach us that there is genuine satisfaction in doing work well. This was not just a ploy to get us to do chores around the house. Many people have discovered for themselves that there is more than satisfaction in achieving excellence in one's work—there is joy.

A salesman talked about the joy he experienced in orchestrating a business deal and seeing it work. The money generated by the deal, he noted, was not nearly as important as the process of making it work. "It was just great to see the parties come together and agree to the deal that would start a new operation," he explained. "Their excitement and the thought of helping create new jobs for people made me feel joyous."

Similarly, Helen, who now owns her own small business, told about the joy she felt as a manager in a very depressing situation. She was responsible for closing down her division when the company for which she worked reduced its operations in order to cut costs. She, along with two hundred others, would lose their jobs. Her final task with the company was to facilitate the process with minimal interruption in the other operations.

Helen decided that in spite of her own anxiety at the prospect of unemployment, she would strive for excellence in her task. That meant, among other things, that she would try to minimize the number of employees who would immediately try to find work elsewhere, thereby jeopardizing a smooth and efficient shutdown. At the same time, she would try to minimize the pain the employees felt over losing their jobs.

In order to achieve her objectives, she developed a plan and took it to the company president. The plan cost the company some money, for it included additional termination benefits to the employees. But the president agreed. The result was everything Helen had hoped for. Only a handful of employees left early. The shutdown did not interfere with other operations. Helen left the company feeling "immense joy" in spite of her own status as an unemployed person. She told us, "I pulled it off. It was one of the best jobs I ever did. At only slight cost to the company, nearly two hundred workers left their jobs feeling pretty good."

Building Your Joy Potential

Whether you seek joy from some kind of personal accomplishment or from work or both, there are a number of things you can do to increase the potential for joyous experiences in the area of achieving.

1. Affirm your capacity to achieve.

Just as you need to affirm your creative potential, you

also need to recognize your ability to achieve. God's people have always struggled with a sense of inadequacy. When God called Moses to lead the people out of the land of Egypt, Moses countered with a series of reasons why he couldn't do it. There was the possibility that the Israelites would not believe or listen to him (Exod. 4:1), and certainly he was not a good speaker (Exod. 4:10). But every "I can't" by Moses was answered with a "you can" by God. For the bottom line was that Moses was sent by God and empowered by God. No child of God is too inept or too powerless to achieve.

For those who doubt their capacity to achieve something, enlightenment may come in a time of crisis, as it did for Moses. Betty was forty-five years old before she was aware of her capacity. A year earlier, her husband had ended their twenty-five-year marriage. With her only child living and working in another country, Betty was alone and feeling very helpless. Her anxiety was only heightened when a man at church offered her a job. "I hadn't worked since high school," she said. "I wasn't sure I could handle any job. And particularly one that required me to use a computer."

Desperate for income, Betty accepted the offer. She checked out books on computer use from the library and stayed up late at night reading them. She stayed late at the office, practicing and learning. Two months later she was a confident woman:

> "At the age of forty-five, I discovered abilities that I did not know I had. I could make it on my own! It was almost like another person took over and was doing a good job with my life. And that person was me! Next to my son, this has been the most joyous experience of my life."

2. Recall your past achievements.
If you doubt your capacity to achieve now, reflect on

your past achievements. There is something in your life that indicates your capacity. It may have been a particularly good essay you wrote in school, or an athletic achievement, or an interpersonal success of some kind. Whatever it was, it underscores the fact that you are able to achieve.

Betty has progressed to another career, which pays more and demands more than her previous job. Sometimes she doubts whether she can handle it well. "But when I start doubting myself," she says, "I go back to that forty-fifth year and my realization that I could make it. And that restores my confidence."

Andrew is a freelance writer who has published widely in magazines and has written copy for in-house business publications. He still suffers the fate of all writers—periodic rejections. "If I get two in a row," he admits, "I start wondering about myself. Maybe I'm no good as a writer after all." To counter his misgivings, he looks at his record of previous writings. He leafs through some copies of published articles. His past achievements lift him up and restore his confidence in his ability.

Self-confidence is a fragile possession at best. When you find yours waning, dig up some past achievements and enjoy them anew. Let them remind you that, like all God's children, you have the capacity to achieve.

3. Be willing to take risks.

As with creating, the willingness to take risks is important to achieving. When you try to be creative or when you try to achieve some goal, you run the risk of falling short, if not of falling flat.

There are other kinds of risks involved in achieving. You may have to take financial and career risks, for example. John left a secure, well-paying management position at the age of thirty-five in order to return to school to become a counselor. He enjoyed his work, but had become increasingly disenchanted with the business world and his career in it. For a number of months he struggled with what he should do. Because he was unmarried, whatever risks he took would be his alone. Still, he didn't want to achieve a new beginning in his life only to discover that it was less satisfying than what he had been doing.

John settled the struggle one night when he was having trouble sleeping. "This is stupid," he told himself. "I'm going to do one thing or the other." He prayed about it, then opted for the new career, and went to sleep. The next day he resigned his position. He didn't even know yet whether he would be accepted into a counseling program at the university. The resignation was a way to seal his commitment to the effort. He recalled:

"During the next few months, I experienced profound states of joy. I was exploring and growing. I had left my life of routine and was reaching for a new level. I also had a few bouts of depression because of the uncertainty of my situation. But when I was accepted for the program, my joy was truly overwhelming. All the risks seemed trivial in the face of that letter of acceptance."

4. Persevere, but . . .

There are many motivational thinkers and writers who urge us to persevere in our efforts. They remind us of such things as the fact that Pearl Buck's famous book *The Good Earth* was turned down by seven publishers and that people laughed at, or even scorned, the initial efforts of many inventors.

Our response is, "Yes, but. . . ." Yes, we agree that you need to persevere, but we are not telling you to persevere on a particular effort to the point of self-destruction. We know a man who decided that he wanted to be a writer.

He showed his work to a number of friends, all of whom tried to gently tell him that he probably should direct his efforts elsewhere. He persevered. For more than fifteen years, he has persevered. He may persevere until death. We hope someone will publish something of his before that time. So far, no one has.

Persevere, but if you are getting nowhere after a reasonable length of time, you probably should try to achieve in some other area. And what is "reasonable"? That's something to decide along with other people who know you and the situation. There is no rule to cover all cases.

Still, persevere. Don't give up too quickly. What if Pearl Buck had stopped submitting her manuscript after five rejections? We know an author who published a successful book that had been turned down by more than twenty publishers!

Achievement without a trail of conquered obstacles behind it is rare, if indeed it exists. Achievement that is unfettered by some initial failures and disappointments is a joyless feat. To achieve and experience the joy of achieving, face the obstacles, work through the failures and disappointments, and persevere until you have attained your goal. As long as you are making some progress, be it ever so agonizingly slow, you have every reason to persevere.

A man who was scheduled to go to Germany wanted to learn enough of the language to speak with the people. Because he did not have much aptitude for foreign languages, he struggled with the class. "At times, the teacher would ask a question in German, and I felt like I had forgotten everything I learned," he said. He thought about giving up, but he persevered. And one day, the breakthrough came. He reflected: "Our teacher began the class with a few sentences in German. And I understood. Not every word. But I actually understood." He raised his hand to respond in German, and the teacher understood him. He'll never speak like a native. It doesn't matter. He knew he would at least be able to communicate to some extent in German. Perseverance paid a dividend of joyous achievement.

6

Experiencing

———◆◆◆———

A n elderly Mexican woman considered it a blessing to say to a departing visitor: "May you go with God, and may nothing new happen to you." To be sure, we experience a certain anxiety when we face the new. It is the anxiety of uncertainty. But the reverse is also true. An American psychiatrist coined the phrase "the trauma of eventlessness" to describe the pain of people for whom there is nothing new and no hope of change. We agree with the implication of the phrase—namely, that humans are creatures who need the emotional and spiritual nourishment of the new.

We Need New Experiences

A social scientist has argued that one of the basic human needs is the need for new experience. We need new experience, he asserted, as much as we need security and recognition. Similarly, the philosopher Alfred North Whitehead noted that humans require something that "absorbs them" for a while, something that is out of the routine of life.

To have new experiences is to follow the pattern of God, who in the ongoing encounter with his creation has continual new experiences. The creation itself was a new experience. And the subsequent history of God's acts in the world, from the covenants to the deliverance of Israel from Egypt to the Incarnation, were a series of new experiences. The history of the world is not the story of an endless round of weary repetition. Rather, it is a story of God engaging humankind with ever-fresh encounters as he leads us on the ultimate journey to the new heaven and new earth.

Since God is at work within each of us, enabling us "both to will and to work for his good pleasure" (Phil. 2:13), God has an endless series of new experiences with each of us as individuals. Reflect upon your own spiritual journey, and think about what it must be like from God's point of view to be dealing with you. When God chose to relate intimately to us, he also chose to be involved in new experiences.

Clearly, the history of God's encounters with humankind is not an unblemished tale of joy. Nor are all of our new experiences likely to be high moments in our lives. Nor, for that matter, is the same experience likely to bring joy to everyone. Some will view a particular new experience with joy, while others may react with a yawn. We stood at the edge of the Grand Canyon and felt a sense of awe and wonder. An acquaintance summed up his experience there with a shrug and these words: "It's just a big hole in the ground."

Although not every new experience will bring you joy, at least some will. And you need these experiences to deliver you from the trauma of *eventlessness* and make more likely the joy of *eventfulness.* The question is, what kind of new experiences? People report experiencing joy in everything from bungee jumping to tasting new foods, but we will focus on four things most often mentioned: nature, travel, moving, and what we call "opening all the stops of your senses."

Experience Nature

"I walked along the beach," one individual told us, "and the sound of the ocean and the feel of the air just pumped up the joy for me." That's a common experience. Most of us can relate to it, even if we seldom are on the beach. The joy of nature is available to all, for it isn't only the magnificence of the ocean that stirs our souls.

What do you feel when you are far from urban lights at night and look up into a star-flooded sky? Without a belief in God, the star-studded heavens can confront us with a sense of aloneness and insignificance. The vast reaches of uncaring matter can mock our longing for meaning. But if, like David, we are aware that "the heavens are telling the glory of God" (Ps. 19:1), then the same experience can be one of joy. As one young woman put it, "I feel joy whenever I walk on a starry night. I see the stars twinkling in various shades of light. And I feel that my being is a part of God's universe."

The young woman's account, incidentally, makes a very important point. Note that she said *whenever*. One of the intriguing things about nature is that what appears on the surface to be a repeated experience can actually be a new experience. Like a good book or a good movie, we never fully assimilate everything the first time. To encounter the stars or the ocean again, therefore, is always to some extent a new experience.

The young woman's account illustrates another important point: You can have a mountaintop experience without climbing to the top of a mountain. Many people, of course, report great joy in experiencing the breathtaking view atop a mountain, but joyous encounters with nature can occur in many ways. People told us about joyous experiences in

- a canoe ride on a lake
- watching backyard trees change color in the fall
- visiting a garden in a city park
- feeling the fresh air of a sunny spring day
- tending a small flower garden
- feeling the wetness of a fine snow blown by the wind

There are a number of reasons why experiences with nature are joyous. First, nature tends to induce a sense of peace and well-being in us. Psychologists have found that just looking at a vase of freshly cut flowers or watching a videotape of a scene from nature can reduce our stress. Joan, a forty-four-year-old teacher, told us that her first encounter with the autumn colors of Vermont brought her an intense feeling of joy and well-being:

"It was nature's final festival before bedding down for the winter. The scenery was almost too beautiful to behold, and my entire being was filled with the richness of life. I remember thinking that if I died at that very moment, it would be okay. Life has been good, and I have been blessed."

Other people have similarly experienced joyous well-being in nature, often as a surprise. A young business-woman recalled a spring day when she walked alone in the Arizona desert:

"I didn't know why I felt so good, but my body felt as if it were going to explode with joy. It was like I could disintegrate and become one with the world. I was right where I was supposed to be, and everything in the world was in its right place at that moment."

Second, experiences with nature are an encounter with God. In the creation we stand before the awesome power of the Creator. And, looking at the creation through the eyes of Christ, we see awesome love as well. Marianne, now the mother of two teenagers, recalled an experience of total joy when she was a teenager herself. She was staying with her parents at a beach house for the summer. One morning, she woke up earlier than usual and decided to go for a swim by herself. She described the experience this way:

> "When I got to the beach I saw the most beautiful ocean I have ever seen in my life. It was motionless. There was no breeze. I stood there watching, transfixed. Everything was so perfect that I felt the presence of God at that moment. It was as if he had created this moment just for me. I remember saying, 'Thank you, God.' "

Third, an encounter with God in nature can be a time of personal renewal. When David looked up at the heavens and contemplated the work of God, he cried out "how majestic is your name in all the earth!" (Ps. 8:1) and noted that God has crowned humans "with glory and honor" (Psalm 8:5). Clearly, his contemplation was a time of personal renewal for him.

Derek was fifty-two when his brother died. He struggled for a long time with the meaning of the premature death. Derek needed renewal. He and his wife took a trip to Yosemite and hiked to the top of Yosemite Falls. As he looked out over the valley, he felt God's renewing power at work in him:

> "It was a prayerful atmosphere, a real haven of rest. The sights and sounds were God's gifts to me. I felt peace. I felt joy. And I felt my faith growing strong as I took in the majesty all around me."

Experiencing

Experience Travel

Most of us are attracted by the notion of travel. In his book *Travels with Charley,* John Steinbeck noted that virtually everyone he talked to was envious of him for spending a year traveling around the nation. Travel is the quintessential new experience. It can take us into new realms of nature. It can expose us to new people and new places. Even a return to the same place is likely to be a new experience. As a man who has frequently visited Niagara Falls said: "Every time I see the Falls, I am once again overwhelmed by their majesty. They never cease to amaze me."

Travel need not involve exotic places to be joyful. "The first real joy I remember," said Lynne, an accountant, "was the summer I went to Florida with my sister and her husband for a week." Lynne was fourteen at the time. It was her first experience of travel, and she had anticipated the trip for weeks. "It was a feeling I had never had before," she recalled. She described how even the drive in the car from her home in Kentucky was joyous: "I remember the change in the landscape, the terrain, seeing palm trees for the first time. Just incredible."

Lynne is thirty-five now, married, with two children. She travels with her family every chance she gets, for she learned an important lesson from the Florida trip:

"For me, it's still a big thrill to take a vacation. Whether it's across the country or just a short distance somewhere. I think it always will be a joyous thing to travel. Every trip is a new and joyous experience. I don't always think of it that way in advance, like I did when I went to Florida. But it happens anyway."

Travel can bring joy in a number of ways. Like Lynne's trip to Florida, the very anticipation of a trip can be joyous. The change of pace, the new sights and sounds, and the stimulation of being in a somewhat different world all tend to generate joy. And the feeling of freedom that comes with travel is often exhilarating. That freedom was expressed by the woman who told of a vacation with her husband: "I felt joyful because I was leaving a lot of responsibilities and pressures behind me, and going off to experience new and exciting things." A man who told of getting lost in Madrid with friends also expressed a feeling of freedom: "I felt free, in a foreign country without responsibility. We were all laughing and enjoying each other's company, even though we were lost. I was as happy as a carefree child."

Don't Be Afraid to Move

Moving to a new location is an obvious way to have new experiences. Yet, like other sources of joy, moving has the potential for distress, if not disaster. A significant number of people who move experience high levels of anxiety and a lack of close friends even after two years in the new location. Unfortunately, many people who move tend to be slow to find a new church home, which exacerbates the problem of isolation and loneliness.

Moving need not be pure trauma. On the contrary, it can be an exciting and joyous experience. Young people often have mixed feelings when they first leave the parental nest, but joy is not an uncommon emotion. A young man told us that, when he left home and moved into his own apartment, he experienced the joy of freedom, of "knowing that I am capable of being alone," and of "proving that I'm a mature person."

It isn't only those who are leaving the parental nest, however, who find moving a joyous experience. Anna lives on the West Coast. She grew up in a town in the Midwest, married a local businessman, and endured thirteen years of a very abusive marriage. In spite of pressure from friends and family to work it out, she divorced her husband.

For the next seven years she worked and supported herself and her daughter. During this time, Anna's ex-husband remarried, and their daughter went away to college. Anna had a problem-free but somewhat dull life. Then she had a career opportunity on the West Coast. She had lived in the Midwest all her life. Most of her family and friends were either in her town or in a bordering state. Not surprisingly, she was reluctant to leave them.

After some anxious thought and prayer, however, Anna decided to make the move. Some of her family and friends were angry with her. They made her feel that she was abandoning them. Anna tried to soothe their hurt but told them that she felt the move was something she had to do. "I can always come back," she told them, "but I may never get another opportunity like this." She was forty-two years old when she moved. It was well over a thousand miles later before the full realization of what she was doing burst into her thoughts:

"I was in Arizona someplace, I guess around Phoenix. And I suddenly realized I was really pulling off the grand move. The geologic grandeur, the bright sun, the overwhelming expanse. It was foreign, but not frightening. I had survived three days on the road, and I knew I was making it. I had tears in my eyes. I wanted to sing hymns. It was wild."

Two years later, Anna is firmly settled in her new home. She is active and happy in her church, is enjoying a new career and a new set of friends, and is confident that the move was God leading her to "a new plane of living." She also has a heightened sense of confidence in her ability to deal with challenges and opportunities in her life.

In saying that she found God leading her, Anna identified the crucial element in a joyous move as opposed to a painful new experience. When the opportunity for the move first came, Anna did not just weigh the financial and friendship advantages and disadvantages. "Financially," she noted, "I would certainly be better off to move. But I wanted to know where God could use me."

Of course, God can use us wherever we are. But keep in mind that God's call to people like Abraham and Moses involved a change of residence. Sometimes God needs us in other places more than where we are. So, to rephrase the quote at the beginning of this chapter, go with God and rejoice in the new experiences he brings to you.

Open All the Stops of Your Senses

Learning to open all the stops of your senses is crucial to new experience. That is, you need to open your eyes, your ears, and your senses of touch and smell to your environment.

Someone once asked Helen Keller what was the worst thing that could happen to a person. She responded that the worst thing is to have vision but not see. To be sure, there are times when we need to be deep in thought about something, but many people are frequently so absorbed in their own thoughts that they miss some joyous new experiences.

When you tune into your environment, you open up the possibility for many new experiences. A medical technician still thinks about an experience of joy she had twenty years earlier. It's an experience she would have missed, even though she was in a stunning, natural setting, if she had not been alert to her surroundings. She was with her family on vacation in a national park. As they began the drive home, she looked around intently to try to capture the beauty in her memory. It was then that she noticed all the flowers:

"I still see them. Their colors. The feeling I had. It was very spiritual. I got tears in my eyes. I asked my husband to stop, and we did so for about ten minutes and just took it all in. I wanted to stay longer, but we had to go. However, the memory continues to bring me joy."

So far, it may sound as if the one requisite for having a new experience is to leave home. Not so. You can gain or miss experiences in or near your home, depending on whether your senses are alert. A husband and wife were taking a nighttime walk around their neighborhood when she exclaimed: "Look. It's a shooting star." He glanced up quickly, but the star was gone. Regrettably, he had missed something he had always wanted to observe. She had seen it, because as they walked, she was watching the skies. He had missed it, because he was absorbed in thoughts about his work.

Lois, an eighty-year-old retired nurse, told us about the joy she experiences daily from the window in her bedroom. For four years, she has watched her environment:

"I see the sky and earth, moonlight and sunlight, corn growing in a nearby field, trees in the distance, a friendly house where parents and children enjoy each other, and a brick church across the street. Each morning, I look out and see God's and man's creation."

The Joy Ride

Lois talked about the joy she experienced in seeing such things as the sun breaking through a "large, black cloud behind the church"; the misty mornings that remind her of days spent in Vermont; winter mornings that frost the evergreens; mornings when the skies open up and "the rain creates its own music"; and mornings with goldfinches at the bird feeder. All such mornings, Lois says, lead her to "join David in his praise of God and know this is the day the Lord has made, and we'll rejoice and be glad in it." Because her eighty-year-old senses are open to her world, Lois experiences, from her bedroom, the primal joy of being alive.

We once saw a movie in which one of the characters was an old man who began each morning by giving God thanks for the gift of life. That sense of joy in just being alive, that joyous gratitude for God's gift of life, is one of the rewards of keeping all the stops of your senses open.

Building Your Joy Potential

Obviously, you can enhance your joy potential by spending time in nature, traveling, moving, and keeping all the stops of your senses open wherever you are. There are a number of other things you can do as well:

1. Commit yourself to trying something new periodically.

Too often, the reason we don't try something new is that we're afraid. If you're afraid, think about the twenty-year-old man who fell in love with sushi, although at first the very thought of raw fish had made him shiver with repugnance. Or think about the woman who tried bungee jumping for the first time at age fifty-eight, and in her exhilaration tried to convince her friends to join her. Or think about Curt, who has spent most of his thirty-six years in a wheelchair because of an injury sustained at birth.

Curt lives by the ocean. He has always been fascinated by the "enchantment of the water," as he described it. In particular, he was intrigued by the world beneath the surface, and he yearned to explore it. His hope seemed pointless, since, as he wryly put it, "I wasn't aware of a wheelchair that could travel under water."

Then Curt met a young woman who scuba dived. She suggested that he might be able to function underwater and offered to be his "power and navigator." After some instruction and difficult training, Curt and his companion descended into the ocean on a sunny August day. He told us about the experience:

"This was joy! It was an intoxicating experience of emotion. There was a mesmerizing quality of silence and serenity under the water. Sounds, colors, and textures created a dance of life for me. When we came out, I felt more complete as a human than I had ever been before."

Keep trying new things. They can lift you to a higher plane of life than you have previously known.

2. Expect a first-time bonus.

When you try something new, prepare yourself for a special sense of exhilaration that often comes with the first time. Many people told us about the special quality of a first-time experience. A woman recalled when her mother took her to a symphony concert for the first time. "I had been taking piano lessons for three years and so hearing Artur Rubenstein play Grieg's Piano Concerto in A minor with the orchestra thrilled me. I was only ten, but I can still remember the joy of that experience. It began a lifelong love affair with music."

Adults can also experience the first-time bonus. One

man told us that seeing the Grand Canyon for the first time created an "upwelling of awe and joy that took my breath away." He said that his reaction was totally unexpected:

"I was absolutely dumbstruck. I couldn't believe what I saw. Nothing I had read, none of the pictures I had seen, prepared me for the sheer magnificence of the sight that lay before me. I could only think that if it affected me that way, what must people have thought who first saw it without even realizing it existed?"

3. Return to the scene of joy.

If you have experienced joy somewhere, return to that place. You can return physically or mentally and thereby reexperience the joy, for we never fully assimilate all the details of an experience. A place of nature can be revisited. A good book can be reread. A good movie can be seen again. Each time you will experience something new.

Some people have a favorite place or experience that is an endless source of joy to them. Diane, a physical therapist, tries to spend some time each summer at a lake in Tennessee. She said:

"When you ask about joy, the lake and the area around it immediately come to mind. I have been overwhelmed by joy when I am there. I feel connected with God and at peace with myself. It's a soul place for me. It renews me. I take in as much each time as my senses can hold."

If you cannot return to such places or experiences in actuality, you can return in memory. Do not underestimate the value of frequent reflection on joyous times of your life. We know that anxiety afflicts people who are haunted by unpleasant events of the past or possible unpleasant happenings in the future. Similarly, well-being can attend those who are stirred by joyous events of the past and who anticipate joyous events of the future. That which occupies your mind will shape your feelings and behavior. That is why Paul wisely told us: "Whatever is true, whatever is honorable, whatever is just, whatever is pure, whatever is pleasing, whatever is commendable, if there is any excellence and if there is anything worthy of praise, think about these things" (Phil. 4:8).

4. Expect joy in the commonplace.

We cannot overstress the point that one need not go to exotic places or have dramatic experiences in order to have joy. Think about the various sources of joy we have discussed in other chapters—such things as family relationships, creative hobbies, and work that is well done.

A mistake many parents make is to think that bringing joy to their children requires them to stretch to the limits of their resources. Joy, like happiness, cannot be purchased. Two stories juxtapose themselves in our minds. One is the father who told us that he was thinking of changing his job—a job that he loved, that enabled him to help people, but that paid him only a moderate salary. Why did he contemplate a change? Because he could not afford to buy his daughter a horse, and she loved horses. He felt that he was depriving her of joy in her life.

The other story is that of a woman who said one of the more joyous times of her life occurred at age fourteen when she went on a vacation with her family. Nothing out of the ordinary happened. "We laughed and listened to an eight-track tape of the Beatles as we drove to the lake," she said. "It was like normal family life. Only we were all together and free to just have fun together."

Not many parents can buy a horse for their daughter. Most parents take their children on some kind of family vacation. Undoubtedly, the horse would have brought joy to the girl, just as the simple family vacation brought joy. The point is, joy is available in the commonplace as well as the unusual. If you can't afford the unusual, you are not thereby deprived of joyous experiences. Look for joy wherever you are. You may be surprised how often you find it.

7

Surrendering

———◆———

Norman Vincent Peale in a sermon once told of a wealthy man who was having trouble sleeping. He went to Dr. Peale because he believed that if he could get near to God, his life would straighten out, and he would be able to sleep. His efforts to get near God, however, had proven fruitless. Perhaps, he suggested, he might finally realize his hope if he gave a lot of money to the church.

Dr. Peale asked him how much he was willing to give. The man named a very large sum. The amount was not large enough, Dr. Peale told him. He would have to give far more; he would have to give himself. Money won't buy God. But when we give ourselves to God, then God gives himself to us.

In essence, the man was in the bargaining mode. Dr. Peale tried to shift him to the surrendering mode. It isn't the people who have struck a bargain with God who find joy; it's those who have surrendered and committed themselves.

To Surrender Is to Live and Rejoice

Surrender is not necessarily a positive word to us. Think about some of its synonyms: *give up, quit, capitu-*

late, concede. Who wants to be a quitter? Haven't we all learned the value of perseverance and of standing on our own two feet? Isn't it a failure to concede?

Nevertheless, what may be a virtue in other realms of life is a disaster in the spiritual realm. And a word that means failure in many ordinary matters means victory in the spiritual. Our surrender to God in Christ is not a loss. It is the triumph of life. It is the affirmation of joy.

Jesus set the pattern for us when he "emptied himself, taking the form of a slave, being born in human likeness. And being found in human form, he humbled himself and became obedient to the point of death—even death on a cross" (Phil. 2:7-8). Jesus surrendered to the call to incarnation. He surrendered to the call to minister rather than be ministered unto. He surrendered to the mob and the authorities who demanded his blood. He did it for "the sake of the joy that was set before him" (Heb. 12:2). And the core of that joy was thrusting open the gates of life for us.

Having modeled surrender for us, Jesus called us to practice it. He told the rich young ruler that he must be willing to give up all for the kingdom of God. He reminded us that those who strive to save their lives will lose them, while those who lose their lives for him will save them (Matt. 16:24). The first disciples who left all to follow him well understood the nature of his call to surrender.

Faith is not at odds with science on the point of surrender. Many social scientists agree that one of the fundamental needs of humans is to become a part of something transcendent. We need to be linked to that which is beyond our own personal pleasure and pain. Researchers tell us that people with meaningful faith are happier, have greater life satisfaction, report higher levels of marital happiness, and tend to be physically and emotionally healthier than those without such faith. Clearly, Jesus' plan for those who surrender—that they "may have life, and have it abundantly" (John 10:10)—begins now and stretches into eternity. No wonder that those who have surrendered rejoice!

But precisely what are the experiences of surrendered people that bring them joy? Those who shared their experiences with us named five things most often: conversion and discipleship—the first acts of surrender; and repentance, prayer, and worship—the ongoing acts of the surrendered person.

Conversion and Discipleship Bring Joy

Encounters with God vary considerably. Some people told us of their joy in being a Christian, but they could not remember one moment or event that marked the surrender. As one man put it:

"I've always believed. I don't ever remember *not* being a Christian. I grew up in a Christian home, with two devoted parents. I was baptized as an infant and nurtured in a Sunday school and confirmed as an adolescent. Never in my life has it occurred to me that I am anything other than a Christian."

Others, however, told about the turning point in their lives when they first encountered God in a conscious and responsive way. In the words of C. S. Lewis, some people are "surprised by joy," coming to faith at an unexpected time—unexpected in the sense that they were neither seeking nor anticipating a spiritual experience. Jerry, a salesman in his thirties, had attended a variety of churches, but had never been baptized and was not really interested in religion when he met a group of people in a campground one summer who were very open and accepting. He was somewhat lonely at the time; some months earlier, he had broken up with a young woman for whom he had deep feelings. He said the relationship "ended very abruptly and with considerable misunderstanding." The people he met at the campground made him feel like a part of their families.

After a few days, some of them told him about their Christian faith. "I was not greatly impressed," he recalled, "but I listened, mainly because they seemed so rational and sincere." When they invited him to visit their church in a nearby town, he decided to attend the services. He told us:

> "As I look back on it, I think it resembles what happened to Paul as he went to Damascus. But the Lord was more gentle with me. I was driving along toward town when I heard a voice say 'He is risen.' That's all. Nothing more. I didn't look around. I knew it might have been my own thoughts coming back to me."

At the church, Jerry found "joy-filled faces, heartwarming music, and sincerity." At the end of the sermon, the pastor invited those present to come to the altar. Jerry described what happened next:

> "I went forward like a child. I didn't understand. I just wanted to believe something. The man who had led the singing pointed out the simple steps in the Bible to let Jesus into my heart. I said, 'yes.' I saw that Jesus was, and had been, knocking at the door of my life. So I let him in. And then came the joy."

Jerry has had times of doubt and times of struggle, but the ten years since that first, unexpected, joyous encounter with faith have been rich with spiritual growth and more experiences of joy.

Note that Jerry mentioned "more experiences." In a

sense, conversion is like a wedding and discipleship is like married life with its ebb and flow of struggles and satisfactions. That is, like a good marriage, committed discipleship brings its own stream of joyous experiences. As a middle-aged man expressed it:

> "I didn't become a Christian until I was in my twenties. It was a high point for me. But I've had a lot of high points since then. Just striving to live as a Christian brings joy. I once interviewed a man who was considering taking a job with our company. He's a high-powered guy, and everyone wanted him to come. Well, he accepted the job, and we became friends. Later, he told me that of all the people he talked with, I was the only one who had been totally honest with him—telling him the problems as well as the potential of the company. It gave me joy to know that I had honored my Lord by trying to be a faithful disciple in that situation."

There are various reasons why conversion and its aftermath of discipleship are so joyous. The fundamental reason, of course, is expressed in the words of the hymn "Amazing Grace": "I once was lost, but now am found." Coming to Christ is coming to life.

Second, one has the sense that he or she has now found the meaning of life. In his novel *Jude the Obscure*, Thomas Hardy wrote that Jude yearned to find something "to anchor on," something to cling to that would give significance to his life. Commitment to Christ does that. It anchors us to meaningfulness. It gives us a sense of direction and purpose. As a woman expressed it:

> "I feel joy that I was privileged to come into this beautiful world. I feel the continual presence of God guiding and protecting me from choosing the wrong fork in the road in decisions I have to make. I firmly believe

that God is in control of my life. And that's the way I want it to be."

Third, the surrendered life means security, the security of God's love. God's promise is that nothing shall cause that love to fail or even to diminish: "I have loved you with an everlasting love; therefore I have continued my faithfulness to you" (Jer. 31:3). Or as Paul reminds us, nothing in all creation "will be able to separate us from the love of God in Christ Jesus our Lord" (Rom. 8:39). People find joy in the fulfillment of that promise in their lives. As a smiling, eighty-five-year-old woman told us: "One of the joys in my life is to know of God's great love for me and to know he is always with me and blesses me with love and peace."

Finally, the surrendered life means that you are never alone. A young father who, along with his wife, had been converted four years earlier, pointed out that they find joy in "knowing that in every circumstance we are not alone. Christ will never leave us or forsake us." At times, he noted, they do not understand the course their lives take, but they know that they can "trust God for the outcome" because God remains true to his promise to never abandon them.

Repentance Brings Joy

To repent, literally, means to turn around, to veer away from the direction one is going and take a different way. As such, repentance is not a once-in-a-lifetime experience but one that occurs many times. We see repentance in Peter's grief after he denied Christ three times. Never again would he deny his Lord; his life took a different direction thereafter. But Peter did not stop repenting. We see him again needing to repent in Acts 10, when a vision from heaven was needed to get him to acknowledge

God's love for Gentiles. Peter did repent, and he went to Cornelius the Gentile with the gospel.

Similarly, when our lives are off course from godliness, we need to repent, to veer into a more Christ-like direction. We may associate grief or guilt or shame with such an experience because of where we have been, but we also will have joy because of where we are going. For repentance is, after all, a veering toward God.

Paul, a college senior, said that he had one of the more joyous experiences of his life when he returned to God "after a long period of running away from him." He felt the joy of coming home. Paul's running from God was probably a form of adolescent rebellion. Reared in a Christian home, he began to question his faith during his first year in college. A psychology professor greatly impressed Paul with his knowledge and his self-confidence about human behavior. The professor was also a religious skeptic and made frequent caustic comments about the Christian faith.

Paul struggled with a growing conflict between his faith and his admiration of the professor's views. His fascination with the subject made him decide to major in psychology during his second semester in school. That decision swayed the balance in his struggle. He stopped going to church and looked to psychological knowledge to give him an understanding of life.

By his senior year, two things had happened that turned Paul back to his faith. One was his realization that, while psychology added a good deal of enriching knowledge to his life, it could not quench his thirst for transcendent meaning in his life. The second thing happened when he was sitting in the class of another psychology professor who was a committed Christian. This professor, who also was very competent and very persuasive, showed Paul that he didn't have to choose between psychology and faith. Paul came home. And his homecoming was joyous. He now says that he is "able to think clearly, to pursue meaningful goals, and to rebuild [his] walk with God."

The joy of repentance may be more difficult to achieve in other kinds of situations. For instance, what about a woman who has an affair, who enjoys it while it lasts, and who finally wants to be restored? One of her hardest tasks may be forgiving herself, and she will not find joy until she is able to do that. Mary Ann, a professional woman in her thirties, knows well the importance of such self-forgiveness. She got involved with a man she met during a business trip. After six months, the affair came to a halt when, after one of her trips, her husband told her that he loved her but felt that she was somehow "distant" from him.

Her husband's affirmation of love forced Mary Ann to confront her situation realistically. She had strong feelings for the man with whom she was having an affair, but these feelings were not as strong as her love for her husband. She broke off the affair. Yet it wasn't enough. She explained:

"I was miserable. I went to my pastor. He told me I needed to confess to God and ask forgiveness. Strangely, I hadn't thought about that. I thought that just stopping the affair was enough. So I did pray for forgiveness, but I still couldn't find release from my guilt. I thought maybe I needed to tell my husband. I went back to my pastor, and we talked a long time. He didn't tell me what to do; however, he did remind me of Jesus and the woman who had been caught in adultery. 'Go, and sin no more.' Christ's words hit me like a brick. 'He *has* forgiven me,' I thought, 'but I haven't forgiven myself.' So I began working on that. I did it by reminding myself daily of that story, and I tried to imagine Jesus saying it to me. One day at breakfast I looked over at my husband, and he smiled at me. I felt a rush of joy. It was finally over. The Lord forgave me. I forgave myself. And it was joyous."

Prayer Brings Joy

A friend told us that her seven-year-old son announced one day that he didn't believe that God answers prayers. As far as he could tell, God hadn't done anything as a result of people praying. His mother, not fully understanding what had produced such skepticism, tried to reassure him. She encouraged him to keep praying and said that she would pray with him each night.

As she put him to bed a week or so later, just before his prayer she told him that he had been a very good boy that day. His eyes opened wide, then he closed them and said: "Thank you, God, for *finally* answering one of my prayers. Mommy said I was good today."

The boy's struggle with the value of prayer is one with which most of us can sympathize. Who has not at times wondered whether there is any point in praying, whether prayer really makes any difference in God's action in the world? We hope we also have shared the boy's experience of the joy of answered prayer.

The point we want to stress here is the joy of prayer, not just the joy of seeing results to our prayers. Indeed, the more joyous experiences of prayer are those in which there is an encounter with God that is meaningful independent of what subsequently happens.

Prayer that is joyful must avoid a number of common deficiencies, each of which revolves around the challenge of making prayer relationship-centered rather than self-centered. One kind of self-centered prayer deficiency occurs when prayer involves little more than asking God for whatever we want. Prayer becomes the presentation of a wish list rather than a presentation of ourselves, an articulation of desires rather than a striving for communion.

It isn't that it is wrong to ask God for what we want. Jesus did that in the garden of Gethsemane when he faced the prospect of death on a cross. But, as always, he put his own desire in the context of his prior commitment to the Father's will: "My Father, if it is possible, let this cup pass from me; yet not what I want but what you want" (Matt. 26:39). Prayer is most joyous when we use it as a way of becoming what God wants us to be rather than as a way to get God to do what we want.

A second kind of self-centered deficiency is when prayer is primarily a sporadic response to crises. There is an old story about a man in a critical situation who began his prayer by saying: "God, as you know, I haven't bothered you now for five years, and if you get me out of this mess I promise not to bother you anymore for another five years." Again, the point is not to refrain from asking God for help in time of crisis, but to make our requests known in the context of an ongoing communion with God, realizing that prayer is far more than a crisis-management tool.

A third deficiency occurs when prayer is mainly a rote spiritual exercise. When done mechanically and mindlessly, the daily repetition of a set of words—even a beautiful set such as the Lord's Prayer—has no joy value. When said thoughtfully and meditatively, repeated prayers may be joyful. The most joy is likely to occur, however, when we also share some spontaneous and fresh thoughts with God.

All these deficiencies reflect self-centered prayer. Whenever prayer is used primarily to get God to act on our behalf, it is little more than a tool of a self-absorbed life. Whenever prayer is practiced like a daily routine such as brushing one's teeth, it is little more than an intrusion in a self-absorbed life. The point is that prayer should be relationship-centered, a time to present ourselves to God and to have some moments of intimacy with him.

Mary is a fifty-year-old university professor who is a surrendered Christian. When asked to relate an experience of joy, she talked about the meaning of prayer in her life:

"Prayer is a joy. It is an experience of God, his overwhelming goodness and forgiveness. God is very real to me then. And it makes all of life a joy. There is a quiet, underlying sense of peace. No matter what!"

For Mary, prayer is not a way to get what she wants, but a way to become what God wants her to be. Prayer is not an attempt to get God to act, but an effort to enjoy quiet moments of intimacy with her Lord. It is not that she never has specific requests. It is, rather, that such requests are made only in the context of an ongoing, prayerful communion with God. The prayerful communion is the matter of fundamental importance. Prayer is joyful for her because it is a time of intimacy in a loving relationship.

Worship Brings Joy

"I was glad when they said to me, 'Let us go to the house of the Lord'" (Ps. 122:1). Worship is joyful, because true worship brings us mindfully into the presence of God. And as David said to God: "You show me the path of life. In your presence there is fullness of joy; in your right hand are pleasures forevermore" (Ps. 16:11).

Joyful worship experiences can occur early in life. Carla, now a naval officer, told about a joyous experience when she was seven. She was scheduled to receive her first communion at the end of the year but decided that she couldn't wait. One Sunday in church she prayed to God, saying that she was "ready *now*":

> "I knew it was right, and I wanted it. I also prayed that God would make it taste like the real thing. I didn't want it to taste like candy just because I was a kid. Well, I knew it was the real thing, because it tasted like cardboard. Everyone was upset when they learned what I had done. But I believe God was excited about it. I still feel joy as I remember how beautiful it was for me."

Like prayer, worship can become a mindless routine. Yet for many Christians, it is more of a regular and joyful time of renewal. And occasionally a church worship service can be a unique experience such as the one that Raymond, a freelance artist, reported.

Some years ago Raymond went to church with his best friend on a morning when both the temperature and the humidity were high. The church was not air-conditioned. Raymond felt hot and uncomfortable, then increasingly bored. He toyed with the notion of just getting up and leaving. Then the choir stood to sing, the congregation was asked to also stand, and within a few minutes Raymond was caught up in an unexpected and strange experience. He described it this way:

> "The choir, which at best was usually mediocre, began to sing in the most beautiful angelic voices. I suddenly felt physically light, cool, and emotionally free. A childlike happiness came over me. I was certain that Jesus was visiting me. My inner voice spoke up and said, 'Jesus, I love you.' "

Raymond's story doesn't have the kind of ending you might expect. Soon, he said, his feelings changed; the choir "returned to singing off-key," and he felt hot and muggy again. Raymond was not strongly religious at the time. He didn't know how to interpret what had happened. His friend did not have the same experience.

Over the years, Raymond remained moderately religious, but the joy of that moment stayed with him. Nothing else in his life quite matched it. Actually, he told us, the experience frightened him because he didn't know how to understand it. But he still can recall the joy, and for that reason he is now opening himself to new spiritual growth. It has taken a good many years, but an unusual, joyful moment of worship is finally leading Raymond into a more committed life.

Another unusual experience of joyful worship was shared with us by a woman who spent nearly ten years looking for a church where she felt at home. Her work led to frequent relocation, which added to the difficulty. She had reached the point where she felt she would spend her entire life searching when, on a crisp autumn Sunday, she attended a new church. She sat in a rear pew, prepared to leave early if the service turned out to be meaningless to her.

As she drank in the words and music, she forgot about herself and her sense of homelessness. She recalled:

"I don't remember exactly what was being said or done. But it seemed as if every cell in my body stood at attention. It felt like I was being personally addressed. As I continued to worship, all the issues that had been plaguing me came into a new perspective. I experienced insight, a clarity of vision that I had never had before."

At the same time, she said her body awakened, "almost like a rush of adrenalin." She began to weep, something she never did in public. There followed what she called "an overwhelming sense of exhilaration, and, at the same time, peace and well-being." At that moment, she said, all the universe seemed to be in its proper place. And she was in her proper place. She had found her home at last.

For some, worship is joyful in a dramatic way. For others, the joy comes in smaller cups. But it comes. Whether the cup of joy is small or large, whether it is partially full or dramatically running over, the important point is that we find joy in worship, in the presence of the living God.

Building Your Joy Potential

As with most matters in human life, surrendering is not an either-or affair. The extent to which we are committed creatures varies from time to time and from situation to situation. When Jesus reminded people that all things are possible to those who believe, the father of the sick boy whom the disciples could not cure cried out: "I believe; help my unbelief!" (Mark 9:24). Similarly, we all can cry out: "I am committed; help my lack of commitment." There are a number of ways we can deepen our commitment and, thereby, increase our joy.

1. Regularly remind yourself of who you are.

When we are caught up in a hectic schedule or absorbed by vexing problems, it is all too easy to forget that we are the children of God. In other words, circumstances can cause us to lose sight of crucial facts: that we have at our disposal all the resources of the Creator of the universe; and that our lives are anchored in, and given meaning and direction by, Jesus Christ.

Scott, a production manager, was in the midst of struggling with a divorce, financial problems, and a new apartment when he had an experience of joy. It came on a day when he reminded himself of who he was. By remembering who he was, he focused on what he still had rather than on what he did not have. He said:

"I had my faith. I had my Savior. I couldn't help but smile, laugh, be grateful. My body felt like singing. I felt God's presence and God's peace. I felt that I was right where I should be. The fear and the stress vanished in the intensity of that experience."

For some people, it is easier to lose sight of who they are when things are going well than when they are under stress. Those who maximize joy remind themselves of who they are in both kinds of circumstances. Paul told the Philippians: "I have learned to be content with whatever I have. I know what it is to have little, and I know what it is to have plenty" (Phil. 4:11-12). This is part of the reason he could rejoice.

2. Regularly renew your commitment.

We are never too close to or too far from God to forgo a renewal of commitment. The people we think of as saints do not consider themselves above the need for renewal. Paul reminded the Philippians that he did not consider himself as one who had reached the end point of spiritual development (Phil. 3:12-13). Rather, he said: "I press on toward the goal for the prize of the heavenly call of God in Christ Jesus" (Phil. 3:14).

It is not a false humility that leads great Christians to disavow their need for continued renewal. It is an awareness of the magnitude of the grace and love of Jesus Christ, before which all of our efforts pale by comparison. Indeed, the magnitude of his grace and love is seen in those at the outer bounds of commitment. As Carrie, now a seminary student in her thirties, discovered when she was twenty-one, the love of Christ can reach to the far country and restore those prodigals who have gone their own way.

Carrie had been raised in a Christian home, but she rebelled in her teens. She wanted to experience more than a Christian commitment seemed to allow. By the age of twenty-one, she was completely out of touch with the Christian community and with any spiritual practices. She was intimately involved with a man who was not a Christian. Then one day she had an experience that changed her life. She can't explain why the experience happened, but she is certain of *what* happened:

> "I was driving in my car. And I began to pray—for the first time in years. I began by saying, 'Hello, God.' Suddenly there was a bright light that seemed to surround and fill the car. I felt God's presence. I felt him welcome me home. At that moment, I was filled with the most incredible peace and joy. I knew that I was loved."

To an outside observer, Carrie may seem to have been out of God's reach when she experienced her renewal. Understandably, she says: "Joy is a gift from God. You don't earn or deserve it." But it is yours when you renew your commitment.

3. Meet regularly with Christian friends.

Did you ever try to keep a single log burning in a fireplace? It's an enormous task. But put a lot of logs together, and they'll keep one another burning without your constant attention. Similarly, the Christian who tries to forge a joyful faith on his or her own will find the task overwhelming. By meeting regularly with others, our faith will both nourish and be nourished. The early disciples knew this and spent time together "day by day" (Acts 2:46). The writer to the Hebrews knew it, and admonished his readers not to neglect assembling together (Heb. 10:25).

Of course, you can meet with Christian friends at times

and places other than church services. Sandy, a Christian mother and housewife, talked about the joy she received from meeting for breakfast with two or three Christian friends each week: "We share the work of God in our lives and request prayer support." She told us how one day she was anxious about whether to allow her teenager to get a driver's license:

"My group ministered to me. They listened, and they spoke with wisdom. I felt as if I was getting good counsel directly from God. I nearly always leave the group feeling loved, guided, and provided for. A sense of joy fills me as I drive home. I feel a sense of love, lightness, and warmth."

4. Serve others in Jesus' name.

Jesus gave us a new standard for leadership: "You know that among the Gentiles those whom they recognize as their rulers lord it over them, and their great ones are tyrants over them. But it is not so among you; but whoever wishes to become great among you must be your servant, and whoever wishes to be first among you must be slave of all" (Mark 10:42-44). The self-serving leaders of this world may find a certain pleasure in their achievements, but only the other-serving leaders of Christ find God's joy. In the parable of the talents, Jesus noted the reward of the two slaves who had served the interests of their master while he was gone: "Enter into the joy of your master" (Matt. 25:21).

An optometrist went with other members of his church to a home for crippled children to entertain as well as talk about Christ. He described it as a particularly joyous experience:

"They were so appreciative of the show, and so receptive to our Christian message. I was blessed just by going there. I was doubly blessed by their responses. And a year later, I could still remember their faces and their movements and feel joyous again."

Like many Christians, this man discovered by experience that it is indeed more blessed to give than to receive. Just as important, he discovered that giving oneself—in spite of a busy schedule—is immensely rewarding. A doctor who gives free care each month to poor people in Mexico, a painting contractor who spends time each month with children in an orphanage, and a mother who gives a few hours each week to visit and minister to people who are in a time of crisis—all talked about the joy, not the burden, of what they do.

Jesus came "not to be served but to serve, and to give his life a ransom for many" (Mark 10:45). He calls us to follow his example, giving ourselves in service to others. When we do, the outcome is not a loss of self but a joyous finding of self.

8

Enhancing Joy: Eleven Principles

urt, the paraplegic we met in chapter 6, told us he now "strives" for joyful experiences. People who are aware of the life-enhancing value of joy do that. In the preceding chapters we have shown you how to increase your joy potential. Here we offer eleven general principles for increasing joy in your life, principles that summarize biblical teachings and encapsulate the Christian experience of joy.

1. Lower Your Awareness Threshold

As we mentioned previously, Helen Keller said that the worst thing that could happen to a person is to have vision but not see. Those who are so wrapped up in their own thoughts and their own concerns that they miss the flow of life around them will miss many joyous experiences.

The apostle John wrote to "the elect lady and her children, . . . I was overjoyed to find some of your children walking in the truth, just as we have been commanded by the Father" (2 John 4). Clearly, John was sufficiently involved with his surroundings to notice and find joy in the children's behavior. Some people might have been with the lady and barely noticed the children. They would have missed the joy.

To lower your awareness threshold, then, means to actively listen and actively watch what is going on around you. It means involvement with life. It means, in the words of a therapist, to let experiences penetrate you. She told about her own experience of joy at a concert where her hair felt like it was standing on end as she resisted every distracting thought and let the music of Mozart penetrate her being. It was a time of unalloyed joy.

2. Remind Yourself of "What Profits"

Jesus may have made the first cost-benefit analysis in history: "For what will it profit them to gain the whole world and forfeit their life?" (Mark 8:36). Realize, in other words, what is truly important and significant for your life. Prioritize on that basis. Since relating is the most common source of joy, invest yourself in relationships. Recall the story of Ty Cobb in chapter 3. What does it profit a man to gain fame and forfeit his relationships?

We have known the joys of relating for a long time. In the Old Testament, people rejoiced at the birth of children (1 Sam. 2), in friendships (1 Sam. 19:1), and in a faithful spouse (Prov. 5:18). John the Baptist rejoiced in Jesus (John 3:29). Jesus rejoiced in his disciples (John 17:13). Over and over again, Paul reminded the early Christians that they were his joy (2 Cor. 7:13; Phil. 4:1; 1 Thess. 2:19-20).

What profits for joy? Surrendering is, of course, the underlying foundation for all joyous experiences. For those who are surrendered, relating is a priority. Creating, achieving, and experiencing are also important. To maximize joy, you need to balance these activities. For instance, achieving can bring joy, but not if it is done at the expense of relating. We recently heard of a man who was offered a job that would bring many rewards from achieving; it also would jeopardize his marriage. He took the job and eventually lost his wife. For joy, it is crucial to remember "what profits."

3. Make Your Emotional Capital Concrete

Emotional capital is the reservoir of strength you build up from joyous experiences (see chapter 2). We suggest you make your emotional capital concrete by writing down all the joyous experiences you can recall. Add to the list as you remember additional experiences and as you have new ones. Periodically review the list and reexperience the joy as you reinforce your emotional capital.

The point is, a joyous experience can have a lifelong payoff for you. An eighty-two-year-old woman shared with us an experience that occurred seventy-two years ago! Her parents gave her a horse on her tenth birthday. "If I close my eyes, I can still see her face, feel her nuzzle me, and remember the joy I felt," she said.

The memories of joyous experiences renew the joy and bring us feelings of well-being. "I thank my God every time I remember you," Paul wrote to the Philippians, "constantly praying with joy in every one of my prayers for all of you" (Phil. 1:3-4). One of the great benefits of joy is that the joys of the past can remain with us and enrich us.

4. Affirm Your Christ-empowered Self

Some Christians confuse humility with self-denigration. Paul, while openly acknowledging his shortcomings and his struggles with himself, also affirmed his Christ-rooted capacity: "I can do all things through him who strengthens me" (Phil. 4:13). Joy comes not to those who despise themselves, but to those who affirm the person created by Christ.

There are two senses in which you need to affirm your Christ-empowered self. One is to affirm your capacity to achieve and to be creative in some way. It is wonderful— if sometimes frustrating or unsettling to parents—to watch infants get to the point where they shrink away from adults and insist: "I can do it by myself." It is sad for adults to lose that sense, to feel powerless in a world of external forces, or to put *a priori* limits on their creative abilities.

Sharon, a homemaker, told us the other sense in which you need to affirm your Christ-empowered self: "Discover your gifts and your loves and follow them." Her point is that there is a certain uniqueness to what brings joy to each of us. She told us how she increases joy in her life:

"I would rather read than see a movie. I would rather travel to new places than return to old, already loved spots. I would rather watch the waves than ski the slopes. I know the things that give me joy."

To accommodate the preferences of family and friends, she sometimes does the "other" things as well, but she says "there is not the same lift to my spirit." Affirm yourself by understanding and, whenever possible, pursuing those things that give you joy.

5. Take Risks

Paul wrote to the Thessalonians, "Yes, you are our glory and joy!" (1 Thess. 2:20). But it is also clear that, for Paul, grounding his joy in those new Christians brought with it a certain amount of agony. Among others, the idlers and busybodies at Thessalonica, the immoral and factious at Corinth, and the quarrelers at Philippi all gave Paul distress. As we have noted a number of times, there are risks to be taken in any potentially joyous experience or situation.

The situation may be a relatively trivial one. Two young women told us their fear of roller coasters. Each hesitated, but finally took the risk of riding a roller coaster at Disneyland. One hated it and nearly got sick (keep in mind that taking risks means that sometimes it won't turn out well!). The other loved it and wanted to ride again.

Risk-taking may also involve a more serious situation. "I don't want to have children," a newly married young woman told us. When we asked why, she replied, "I just don't think I would be a good mother. I don't think I have the patience needed." The young woman loved children but doubted her capacity for patience. She was afraid to take the risk.

Her husband badly wanted children, however, so two years later she agreed to "give it a try." We didn't see her for a number of years and then met by chance. She now had not one but two children. "How do you enjoy being a mother?" we asked. The glowing smile that came over her face told us the answer even before she spoke. She was very grateful that she had taken the risk.

6. Practice Gratitude

"Rejoice always, pray without ceasing, give thanks in all circumstances" (1 Thess. 5:16-17). The three commands are not separable. We'll address the topics of prayer and other spiritual exercises later. Here we want to concentrate on giving thanks.

It is a joyless exercise to focus on what you don't have or on how little you have in comparison to someone else. Joy is nurtured by gratitude. You can practice gratitude, even if it is in tentative form: "God, I don't feel grateful at this moment, but in accord with your command I give you thanks for. . . ." Whatever our present circumstances, there is always something for which we can give thanks.

For instance, have you ever given God thanks simply for being alive? A man who has had his share of pain, including the premature death of a beloved first wife, told us that he finds joy "just in being alive and knowing that God takes care of us."

Another man, who told us he is joyous "*a lot,*" gave us his formula:

> "I make an effort each day to think of all the wonderful things in my life and thank God for them. My life is blessed partly due to the fact that I really *do* make an effort to appreciate all the good things in it."

Gratitude easily blossoms into joy.

7. Look for Joy in the Small Things

The idea that "small is beautiful" stresses the fact that life can be good without being lavish. The idea that small can be joyous stresses the fact that joy comes from the little things in life as well as from the dramatic and the momentous. Paul was eager to send Epaphroditus back to Philippi, knowing that they would "rejoice at seeing him again" (Phil. 2:28). There was nothing particularly dramatic or momentous about the return of a fellow Christian, even one who had been extremely ill. But, as Paul knew, such small events can be sources of joy.

Sometimes it may take a dramatic event to make us appreciate the small. Mac is only in his twenties, but, like Epaphroditus, he has already experienced a life-threatening illness. Since his recovery, Mac has a new perspective on life. "I get small bits of joy in routine events," he explained. "I appreciate things I used to think of as trivial. God has given me the gift of life, and I'm enjoying every part of it now."

Others may learn to appreciate the small without such drama. A young woman told us the most important lesson she ever learned: "Joy doesn't come from external things, but from your attitude about them. I get joy from simple things, like a sunset, a starry night, and being with friends."

8. Play It Straight

David also knew that he had to play life straight—that is, that he had to be true to God. When the prophet Nathan confronted him about his sins against Bathsheba and Uriah, he knew that only God's cleansing forgiveness could restore joy to his life. After confessing his sin and praying for forgiveness, he said to God: "Restore to me the joy of your salvation" (Ps. 51:12).

David discovered that he couldn't have it both ways. He couldn't indulge his lust and still have the joy of God's salvation. We have known people who were willing to identify themselves as Christian as long as it didn't interfere too much with what they wanted to do. We have not found such people to be filled with joy.

We should, as Paul wrote, "live lives that are self-controlled, upright, and godly" (Titus 2:12). To some people, that sounds like the death of fun. Actually, it is a call to joy. As a man told us: "I was tempted once to be unfaithful to my wife. I resisted, thank God. I now know the joy of a faithful marriage."

9. Nurture Your Spiritual Life

There is joy in God's word (Ps. 19:8; Jer. 15:16). There is joy in giving (Mal. 3:10; 2 Cor. 8). There is joy in worship (Ps. 27:6; Acts 2:46-47). In essence, there is joy to be found in the rituals of faith. Rightly practiced, they are not obligations to be fulfilled but experiences in which to rejoice. When you nurture your spiritual life you are, at the same time, cultivating joy in your life. By *nurture* we mean regular spiritual exercises. In the words of Brother Lawrence, we need to do those things that enable us to "practice the presence of God." The more you are aware of God's presence in your day, the more it will be a day of rejoicing.

One woman told us she feels some joy every day, and her joy is rooted in God "and the presence of the Holy Spirit." A man noted that he feels joy "during meditation and while singing songs of praise to God." Sandy, a mother who meets regularly with Christian friends (chapter 7), cannot recall any experience of joy before she was thirty-five, when she "experienced God in a new, loving, and personal way." Now joy is frequent, particularly when she meets with her friends and when she is "alone with God, praying, praising, reading his word, or listening to him with my soul."

Sandy doesn't experience joy *every* time she does these things; it won't likely happen every time for you either. However, joy will come with sufficient frequency to make spiritual nurture a priority in your life.

10. Engage in Ministry

When the seventy returned from the mission on which Jesus had sent them, they joyously told of what they had accomplished in his name (Luke 10:17). Every Christian needs to know the joy of engaging in ministry. Your ministry may be in your church—in some kind of mission or fellowship group—or it may be outside the church.

In finding a ministry, it is important to remember the law of the least. Jesus formulated the law in his portrayal of judgment. The righteous will ask him when they ever ministered directly to Jesus by giving him food, drink, clothing, shelter, or comfort. And his answer is this: "Truly I tell you, just as you did it to one of the least of these who are members of my family, you did it to me" (Matt. 25:40).

The point is, we serve our Lord by serving others. We know people who rejoice in everything from teaching Sunday school, to taking food and clothing to an orphanage, to participating in an outreach program for those in crisis, to building a Christian atmosphere in the workplace. The possibilities are endless because the needs are numberless. Yet whatever you do for others in the name of Christ will enhance the probability of joy in your life. As St. John of the Cross wrote, those who serve God swim in joy and are always in the mood for singing.

11. Keep Trying Until You Sing

Have you noticed the "ing-ness" of our chapter headings in part 2? It is not relationships, but relating; not creativity, but creating; and so on. We want to stress the "ing-ness" of life, because that is God's way of acting. We could capture more accurately the meaning of Paul's words to the Philippians that God is at work in us by translating it this way: "For it is God who keeps on working in you" (2:13).

In other words, God doesn't give up on us when we don't turn out perfect the first time. Neither should we give up if, for example, we take the risk and establish a relationship and it turns out to be more painful than joyous. Keep relating. The joy will come.

David knew the importance of perseverance in the area of surrendering. He knew both the joy of God's presence and the horror of God's seeming absence from his life. And when he was in spiritual darkness, he knew that if he kept seeking God, he would eventually find him and sing again of his goodness. If you reach a point where you think that the joy and peace of God's salvation will always remain just beyond your grasp, remember David's words and continue your quest:

> How long, O LORD? Will you forget me forever?
> How long will you hide your face from me?
>
> ....
>
> But I trusted in your steadfast love;
> my heart shall rejoice in your salvation.
> I will sing to the LORD,
> because he has dealt bountifully with me.
>
> (Ps. 13:1, 5-6)